Light for Students

Compiled from the writings of
Sri Aurobindo and the Mother

SRI AUROBINDO SOCIETY
PONDICHERRY, INDIA

First edition 1978
Eighth impression 1998
Second edition 2002
Reprinted 2004, 2006, 2008

Rs. 55
ISBN 978-81-7060-189-0

Compiled by Vijay
Published by Sri Aurobindo Society,
Pondicherry 605 002
Web   http://www.sriaurobindosociety.org.in

Printed at Sri Aurobindo Ashram Press, Pondicherry
PRINTED IN INDIA

One of the most important periods in the life of an individual is the time he spends as a student. During this period his personality develops and takes shape determining to a great extent the course of his future.

This booklet brings together some selected passages from the writings of Sri Aurobindo and the Mother which we feel can be of great help to a student in organising most of the important aspects of his study and life.

The passages from Sri Aurobindo are in the original English; most of the passages from the Mother (selections from her talks and writings) are translations from the original French.

Every compilation in its very nature is likely to have a personal and subjective approach, and though here a sincere attempt has been made to be faithful to the vision of Sri Aurobindo and the Mother, the compiler accepts his responsibility.

We hope that this booklet will help its readers to become conscious of their aim in life and the work they have to do and will inspire them to prepare themselves for it and to strive towards an ever greater perfection.

"O TRUTH, COME, MANIFEST."

आयाहि सत्य आविर्भव।

Contents

Sri Aurobindo at the age of eleven

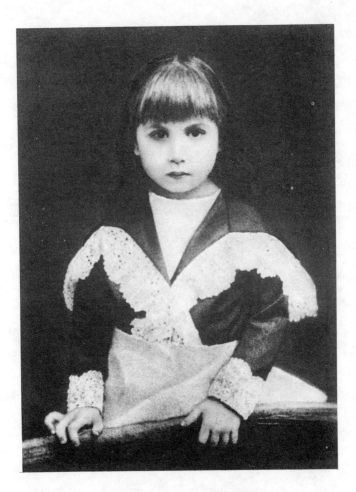

The Mother at the age of seven

A Call to Young India

Sri Aurobindo:

... There are times in a nation's history when Providence places before it one work, one aim, to which everything else, however high and noble in itself, has to be sacrificed. Such a time has now arrived for our Motherland when nothing is dearer than her service, when everything else is to be directed to that end. If you will study, study for her sake; train yourselves body and mind and soul for her service. You will earn your living that you may live for her sake. You will go abroad to foreign lands that you may bring back knowledge with which you may do service to her. Work that she may prosper. Suffer that she may rejoice. All is contained in that one single advice.

*

...Our endeavour shall be to prepare the paths and to accomplish the beginning of a great and high change which we believe to be and aim at making the future of the race and the future of India. Our ideal is a new birth of humanity into the spirit; our life must be a spiritually inspired effort to create a body of action for that great new birth and creation.

A spiritual ideal has always been the characteristic idea and aspiration of India. But the progress of Time and the need of humanity demand a new orientation and another form of that ideal. The old forms and methods are no longer sufficient for the purpose of the Time-Spirit. India can no longer fulfil herself on lines that are too narrow for the great steps she has to take in the future. Nor is ours the spirituality of a life that is aged and world-weary and burdened with the sense of the illusion and miserable inutility of all God's mighty creation. Our ideal is not the spirituality that withdraws from life but the conquest of life by the power of the spirit. It is to accept the world as an effort of manifestation of the Divine, but also to transform humanity by a greater effort of manifestation than has yet been accomplished, one in which the veil between man and God shall be removed, the divine manhood of which we are capable shall come to birth and our life shall be remoulded in the truth and light and power of the spirit. It is to make of all our action a sacrifice to the master of our action and an expression of the greater self in man and of all life a Yoga....

This secret too has been possessed but not sufficiently practised by India. It is summarised in the rule of the Gita, *yogasthaḥ kuru karmāṇi.* Its principle is to do all actions in Yoga, in union with God, on the foundation of the highest self and through the rule of all our members by the power of the spirit. And this we believe to be not only possible for man but the true solution of all his problems and difficulties. This then is the message we shall constantly utter and this the ideal that we shall put before the young and rising India, a spiritual life that shall take up all human activities and avail to transfigure the world for the great age that is coming. India, she that has carried in herself from of old the secret, can alone lead the way in this great transformation of which the present *sandhyā* of the old *yuga* is the forerunner. This must be her mission and service to humanity, – as she discovered the inner spiritual life for the individual, so now to discover for the race its integral collective expression and found for mankind its new spiritual and communal order.

Our first object shall be to declare this ideal: insist on the spiritual change as the first necessity and group together all who accept it and are ready to strive sincerely to fulfil it: our second shall be to build up not only an individual but a communal life on this principle. An outer activity as well as an inner change is needed and it must be at once a spiritual, cultural, educational, social and economical action. Its scope, too, will be at once individual and communal, regional and national, and eventually a work not only for the nation but for the whole human people. The immediate (?) of this action will be a new creation, a spiritual education and culture, and enlarged social spirit founded not on division but on unity, on the perfect growth and freedom of the individual, but also on his unity with others and his dedication to a larger self in the people and in humanity, and the beginning of an endeavour towards the solution of the economic problem founded not on any western model but on the communal principle native to India.

Our call is to young India. It is the young who must be the builders of the new world, – not those who accept the competitive individualism, the capitalism or the materialistic communism of the West as India's future ideal, not those who are enslaved to old religious formulas and cannot believe in the acceptance and transformation of life by the spirit, but all who are free in mind and heart to accept a completer truth and labour for a greater ideal. They must be men who will dedicate themselves not to the past or the present but to the future. They will need to consecrate their lives to an exceeding of their lower self, to the realisation of God in themselves and in all human beings and to a whole-minded and indefatigable labour for the nation and for humanity. This ideal can be as yet only a little seed and the life that embodies it a small nucleus, but it is our fixed hope that the seed will grow into a great tree and the nucleus be the heart of an ever-extending formation. It is with a confident trust in the spirit that inspires us that we take our place among the standard-bearers of the new humanity that is struggling to be born amidst the chaos of a world in dissolution, and of the future India, the greater India of the rebirth that is to rejuvenate the mighty outworn body of the ancient Mother.

*

We say to the individual and especially to the young who are now arising to do India's work, the world's work, God's work: "You cannot cherish these ideals, still less can you fulfil them if you subject your minds to European ideas or look at life from the material standpoint. Materially you are nothing, spiritually you are everything. It is only the Indian who can believe everything, dare everything, sacrifice everything. First, therefore, become Indians. Recover the patrimony of your forefathers. Recover the Aryan thought, the Aryan discipline, the Aryan character, the Aryan life. Recover the Vedanta, the Gita, the Yoga. Recover them not only in intellect or sentiment but in your lives. Live them and you will be great and strong, mighty, invincible and fearless. Neither life nor death will have any terrors for you. Difficulty and impossibility will vanish from your vocabularies. For it is in the spirit that strength is eternal and you must win back the kingdom of yourselves, the inner Swaraj, before you can win back your outer empire. There the Mother dwells and She waits for worship that She may give strength. Believe in Her, serve Her, lose your wills in Hers, your egoism in the greater ego of the country, your separate selfishness in the service of humanity. Recover the source of all strength in yourselves and all else will be added to you, social soundness, intellectual pre-eminence, political freedom, the mastery of human thought, the hegemony of the world."

*

The Mother:

Let India work for the future and set the example. Thus she will recover her true place in the world.

Since long it was the habit to govern through division and opposition.

The time has come to govern through union, mutual understanding and collaboration.

To choose a collaborator, the value of the man is more important than the party to which he belongs.

The greatness of a country does not depend on the victory of a party but on the union of all the parties.

*

Youth does not depend on the small number of years one has lived, but on the capacity to grow and to progress. To grow is to increase one's potentialities, one's capacities; to progress is to make constantly more perfect the capacities that one already possesses. Old age does not come from a great number of years but from the incapacity or the refusal to continue to grow and progress. I have known old people of twenty and young people of seventy. As soon as one wants to settle down in life and reap the benefits of one's past efforts, as soon as one thinks that one has done what one had to do and accomplished what one had to accomplish, in short, as soon as one ceases to progress, to advance along the road of perfection, one is sure to fall back and become old.

*

As soon as you stop advancing, as soon as you stop progressing, as soon as you cease to better yourself, cease to gain and grow, cease to transform yourself, you truly become old, that is to say, you go downhill towards disintegration.

There are young people who are old and there are old people who are young. If you carry in you this flame for progress and transformation, if you are ready to leave everything behind so that you may advance with an alert step, if you are always open to a new progress, a new improvement, a new transformation, then you are eternally young. But if you sit back satisfied with what has been accomplished, if you have the feeling that you have reached your goal and you have nothing left to do but enjoy the fruit of your efforts, then already more than half your body is in the tomb: it is decrepitude and the true death.

Everything that has been done is always nothing compared with what remains to be done.

Do not look behind. Look ahead, always ahead and go forward always.

The Ideal

The Mother:

There is an ascending evolution in nature which goes from the stone to the plant, from the plant to the animal, from the animal to man. Because man is, for the moment, the last rung at the summit of the ascending evolution, he considers himself as the final stage in this ascension and believes there can be nothing on earth superior to him. In that he is mistaken. In his physical nature he is yet almost wholly an animal, a thinking and speaking animal, but still an animal in his material habits and instincts. Undoubtedly, nature cannot be satisfied with such an imperfect result; she endeavours to bring out a being who will be to man what man is to the animal, a being who will remain a man in its external form, and yet whose consciousness will rise far above the mental and its slavery to ignorance.

Sri Aurobindo came upon earth to teach this truth to men. He told them that man is only a transitional being living in a mental consciousness, but with the possibility of acquiring a new consciousness, the Truth-consciousness, and capable of living a life perfectly harmonious, good and beautiful, happy and fully conscious. During the whole of his life upon earth, Sri Aurobindo gave all his time to establish in himself this consciousness he called supramental, and to help those gathered around him to realise it.

*

An aimless life is always a miserable life.

Every one of you should have an aim. But do not forget that on the quality of your aim will depend the quality of your life.

Your aim should be high and wide, generous and disinterested; this will make your life precious to yourself and to others.

But whatever your ideal, it cannot be perfectly realised unless you have realised perfection in yourself.

*

Human beings could be classified under four principal categories according to the attitude they take in life:

1) Those who live for themselves. They consider everything in relation to themselves and act accordingly. The vast majority of men are like this.

2) Those who give their love to another human being and live for him. As for the result, everything naturally depends on the person one chooses to love.

3) Those who consecrate their life to the service of humanity through some activity done not for personal satisfaction but truly to be useful to others without calculation and without expecting any personal gain from their work.

4) Those who give themselves entirely to the Divine and live only for Him and through Him. This implies making the effort required to find the Divine, to be conscious of His Will and to work exclusively to serve Him.

In the first three categories, one is naturally subject to the ordinary law of suffering, disappointment and sorrow.

It is only in the last category — if one has chosen it in all sincerity and pursued it with an unfailing patience — that one finds the certitude of total fulfilment and a constant luminous peace.

*

Essentially there is but one single true reason for living: it is to know oneself. We are here to learn – to learn what we are, why we are here, and what we have to do. And if we don't know that, our life is altogether empty – for ourselves and for others.

And so, generally, it is better to begin early, for there is much to learn. If one wants to learn about life as it is, the world as it is, and then really know the why and the how of life, one can begin when very young, from the time one is very, very tiny – before the age of five. And then, when one is a hundred, he will still be able to learn. So it is interesting. And all the time one can have surprises, always learn something one didn't know, meet with an experience one did not have before, find something one was ignorant of. It is surely very interesting. And the more one knows, the more aware does one become that one has everything to learn.

*

We should never tell ourselves, openly or indirectly, "I want to be great, what vocation can I find for myself in order to become great?"

On the contrary, we should tell ourselves, "There must certainly be something I can do better than anyone else, since each one of us is a special mode of manifestation of the divine power which, in its essence, is one in all. However humble and modest it may be, this is precisely the thing to which I should devote myself, and in order to find it, I shall observe and analyse my tastes, tendencies and preferences, and I shall do it without pride or excessive humility, whatever others may think I shall do it just as I breathe, just as the flower smells sweet, quite simply, quite naturally, because I cannot do otherwise."

What should be our Attitude

The Mother:

People sleep, they forget, they take life easy – they forget, forget all the time.... But if we could remember... that we are at an exceptional hour, a *unique* time, that we have this immense good fortune, this invaluable privilege of being present at the birth of a new world, we could easily get rid of everything that impedes and hinders our progress.

So, the most important thing, it seems, is to remember this fact; even when one doesn't have the tangible experience, to have the certainty of it and faith in it; to remember always, to recall it constantly, to go to sleep with this idea, to wake up with this perception; to do all that one does with this great truth as the background, as a constant support, this great truth that we are witnessing the birth of a new world.

We can participate in it, we can become this new world. And truly, when one has such a marvellous opportunity, one should be ready to give up everything for its sake.

*

You are to be conscious of yourself, you must awake to your nature and movements, you must know why and how you do things or feel or think them; you must understand your motives and impulses, the forces, hidden and apparent, that move you; in fact, you must, as it were, take to pieces the entire machinery of your being. Once you are conscious, it means that you can distinguish and sift things, you can see which are the forces that pull you down and which help you

on. And when you know the right from the wrong, the true
from the false, the divine from the undivine, you are to act
strictly up to your knowledge; that is to say, resolutely reject
one and accept the other. The duality will present itself at
every step and at every step you will have to make your choice.

*

*"To know oneself and control oneself", what does this
mean?*

This means to be conscious of one's inner truth, conscious
of the different parts of one's being and their respective functions. You must know why you do this, why you do that; you
must know your thoughts, know your feelings, all your activities, all your movements, of what you are capable, etc.
And to know oneself is not enough: this knowledge must
bring a conscious control. To know oneself perfectly is to
control oneself perfectly.

But there must be an aspiration at every moment.

It is never too early to begin, never too late to continue.
That is, even when you are quite young, you can begin to
study yourself and know yourself and gradually to control
yourself. And even when you are what is called "old", when
you are quite aged, it is not too late to make the effort to
know yourself better and better and control yourself better
and better. That is the Science of Living.

To perfect oneself, one must first become conscious of
oneself. I am sure, for instance, that the following situation
has arisen many times in your life: someone asks you suddenly, "Why have you done that?" Well, the spontaneous

reply, is, "I don't know." If someone asks you, "What are you thinking of?" you reply, "I don't know." "Why are you tired?" – "I don't know." "Why are you happy?" – "I don't know," and so on. I can take indeed fifty people and ask them suddenly, without preparation, "Why have you done that?" and if they are not inwardly "awake", they will all answer, "I don't know" (of course I am not speaking here of those who have practised a discipline of self-knowledge and of following up their movements to their extreme limits; these people can, naturally, collect themselves, concentrate and give the right answer, but only after a little while). You will see that it is like that if you look well at your whole day. You say something and you don't know why you say it – it is only after the words are out of your mouth that you notice that this was not quite what you wanted to say. For instance, you go to see someone, you prepare beforehand the words you are going to speak, but once you are in front of the person in question, you say nothing or it is other words which come from your mouth. Are you able to say to what extent the atmosphere of the other person has influenced you and stopped you from saying what you had prepared? How many people can say that? They do not even observe that the person was in such or such a state and that it was because of this that they could not tell him what they had prepared. Of course, there are very obvious instances when you find people in such a bad mood that you can ask nothing of them. I am not speaking of these. I am speaking of the clear perception of reciprocal influences: what acts and re-acts on your nature; it is this one does not have. For example, one becomes suddenly uneasy or happy, but how many people can say, "It is this"? And it is difficult to know, it is not at all easy. One must be quite "awake"; one must be constantly in a very attentive state of observation.

There are people who sleep twelve hours a day and say the rest of the time, "I am awake"! There are people who sleep twenty hours a day and the rest of the time are but half awake!

To be in this state of attentive observation, you must have, so to say, antennae everywhere which are in constant contact with your true centre of consciousness. You register everything, you organise everything and, in this way, you cannot be taken unawares, you cannot be deceived, mistaken, and you cannot say anything other than what you wanted to say. But how many people normally live in this state? It is this I mean, precisely, when I speak of "becoming conscious". If you want to benefit most from the conditions and circumstances in which you find yourself, you must be fully awake: you must not be taken by surprise, you must not do things without knowing why, you must not say things without knowing why. You must be constantly awake.

You must also understand that you are not separate individualities, that life is a constant exchange of forces, of consciousness, of vibrations, of movements of all kinds. It is as in a crowd, you see: when everyone pushes all go forward, and when all recede, everyone recedes. It is the same thing in the inner world, in your consciousness. There are all the time forces and influences acting and re-acting upon you, it is like a gas in the atmosphere, and unless you are quite awake, these things enter into you, and it is only when they have gone well in and come out as if they came from you, that you become aware of them. How many times people meet those who are nervous, angry, in a bad mood, and themselves become nervous, angry, moody, just like that, without quite knowing why. Why is it that when you play against certain people you play very well, but when you play against others you cannot play? And those very quiet people, not at all wicked, who suddenly become furious when they are in a furious crowd! And no one knows who has started it: it is something that went past and swept off the consciousness. There are people who can let out vibrations like this and others respond without knowing why. Everything is like that, from the smallest to the biggest things.

To be individualised in a collectivity, one must be absolutely conscious of oneself. And of which self? – the self which is above all intermixture, that is, what I call the truth of your being. And as long as you are not conscious of the Truth of your being, you are moved by all kinds of things, without taking any note of it at all. Collective thought, collective suggestions are a formidable influence which act constantly on individual thought. And what is extraordinary is that one does not notice it. One believes that one thinks "like that", but in truth it is the collectivity which thinks "like that". The mass is always inferior to the individual. Take individuals with similar qualities, of similar categories, well, when they are alone these individuals are at least two degrees better than people of the same category in a crowd. There is a mixture of obscurities, a mixture of unconsciousness, and inevitably you slip into this unconsciousness. To escape this there is but one means: to become conscious of oneself, more and more conscious and more and more attentive.

Try this little exercise: at the beginning of the day, say: "I won't speak without thinking of what I say." You believe, don't you, that you think all that you say! It is not at all true, you will see that so many times the word you do not want to say is ready to come out, and that you are compelled to make a conscious effort to stop it from coming out.

I have known people who were very scrupulous about not telling lies, but all of a sudden, when together in a group, instead of speaking the truth they would spontaneously tell a lie; they did not have the intention of doing so, they did not think of it a minute before doing it, but it came "like that". Why? – because they were in the company of liars; there was an atmosphere of falsehood and they had quite simply caught the malady!

It is thus that gradually, slowly, with perseverance, first of all with great care and much attention, one becomes conscious, learns to know oneself and then to become master of oneself.

*

And it is there we have the solution of the problem. You can at every minute make the gift of your will in an aspiration – and an aspiration which formulates itself very simply, not just "Lord, Thy will be done", but "Grant that I may do as well as I can the best thing to do."

You may not know at every moment what is the best thing to do nor how to do it, but you can place your will at the disposal of the Divine to do the best possible, the best thing possible. You will see it will have marvellous results. Do this with consciousness, sincerity and perseverance, and you will find yourself getting along with gigantic strides. It is like that, isn't it? One must do things with all the ardour of one's soul, with all the strength of one's will; do at every moment the best possible, the best thing possible. What others do is not your concern — this is something I shall never be able to repeat to you often enough.

Never say, "So-and-so does not do this", "So-and-so does something else", "That one does what he should not do" – all this is not your concern. You have been put upon earth, in a physical body, with a definite aim, which is to make this body as conscious as possible, make it the most perfect and most conscious instrument of the Divine. He has given you a certain amount of substance and of matter in all the domains – mental, vital and physical – in proportion to what He expects from you, and all the circumstances around you are also in proportion to what He expects of you, and those who tell you, "My life is terrible, I lead the most miserable life in the world", are donkeys! Everyone has a life appropriate to his total development, everyone has experiences which help him in his total development, and everyone has difficulties which help him in his total realisation.

If you look at yourself carefully, you will see that one always carries in oneself the opposite of the virtue one has to realise (I use "virtue" in its widest and highest sense). You have a special aim, a special mission, a special realisation which is your very own, each one individually, and you carry in yourself all the obstacles necessary to make your realisation perfect. Always you will see that within you the shadow and the light are equal: you have an ability, you have also the negation of this ability. But if you discover a very black hole, a thick shadow, be sure there is somewhere in you a great light. It is up to you to know how to use the one to realise the other.

This is a fact very little spoken about, but one of capital importance. And if you observe carefully you will see that it is always thus with everyone. This leads us to statements which are paradoxical but absolutely true; for instance, that the greatest thief can be the most honest man (this is not to encourage you to steal, of course!) and the greatest liar can be the most truthful person. So, do not despair if you find in yourself the greatest weakness, for perhaps it is the sign of the greatest divine strength. Do not say, "I am like that, I can't be otherwise." It is not true. You are "like that" because, precisely, you ought to be the opposite. And all your difficulties are there just that you may learn to transform them into the truth they are hiding.

Once you have understood this, many worries come to an end and you are very happy, very happy. If one finds one has very black holes, one says, "This shows I can rise very high", if the abyss is very deep, "I can climb very high."

*

There are some very wise recommendations here, for example, not to concern oneself with what others do nor with the mistakes they make, but to attend to one's own faults and negligences and rectify them. Another wise counsel is never to utter too many eloquent words which are not effectuated in action – speak little, act well. Beautiful words, they say, that are mere words, are like flowers without fragrance.

And finally, lest you get discouraged by your own faults, the Dhammapada gives you this solacing image: the purest lily can spring out of a heap of rubbish by the wayside. That is to say, there is nothing so rotten that it cannot give birth to the purest realisation.

Whatever may be the past, whatever may be the faults

committed, whatever the ignorance in which one might have lived, one carries deep within oneself the supreme purity which can translate itself into a wonderful realisation.

The whole point is to think of that, to concentrate on that and not to be concerned with all the difficulties and obstacles and hindrances.

Concentrate exclusively on what you want to be, forget as entirely as possible what you do not want to be.

*

Give up all personal seeking for comfort, satisfaction, en-joyment or happiness. Be only a burning fire for progress, take whatever comes to you as an aid to your progress and immediately make whatever progress is required.

Try to take pleasure in all you do, but never do anything for the sake of pleasure.

Never get excited, nervous or agitated. Remain perfectly calm in the face of all circumstances. And yet be always alert to discover what progress you still have to make and lose no time in making it.

Never take physical happenings at their face value. They are always a clumsy attempt to express something else, the true thing which escapes our superficial understanding.

Never complain of the behaviour of anyone, unless you have the power to change in his nature what makes him act in this way; and if you have the power, change him instead of complaining.

Whatever you do, never forget the goal which you have set before you.

How to Study

The Mother:

Can one study for the Divine and not for onself, prepare oneself for the divine work?

Yes, if you study with the feeling that you must develop yourselves to become instruments. But truly, it is done in a very different spirit, isn't it? – very different. To begin with, there are no longer subjects you like and those you don't, no longer any classes which bore you and those which don't, no longer any difficult things and things not difficult, no longer any teachers who are pleasant or any who are not – all that disappears immediately. One enters a state in which, whatever happens one takes as an opportunity to learn to prepare oneself for the divine work, and everything becomes interesting. Naturally, if one is doing that, it is quite all right.

*

You see, my child, the unfortunate thing is that you are too preoccupied with yourself. At your age I was exclusively occupied with my studies – finding things out, learning, understanding, knowing. That was my interest, even my passion. My mother, who loved us very much – my brother and myself – never allowed us to be ill tempered or discontented or lazy. If we went to complain to her about one thing or another, to tell her that we were discontented, she would make fun of us or scold us and say, "What is this nonsense? Don't be ridiculous. Quick! off you go and work, and never mind

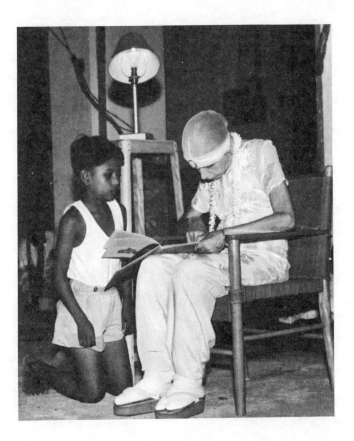

The Mother telling a story

whether you are in a good or a bad mood! That is of no interest at all."

My mother was perfectly right and I have always been very grateful to her for having taught me the discipline and the necessity of self-forgetfulness through concentration on what one is doing.

I have told you this because the anxiety you speak of comes from the fact that you are far too concerned about yourself. It would be better for you to pay more attention to what you are doing and to do it well (painting or music), to develop your mind, which is still very uncultivated, and to learn the elements of knowledge which are indispensable to a man if he does not want to be ignorant and uncultured.

If you worked regularly eight to nine hours a day, you would be hungry and you would eat well, you would feel sleepy and sleep peacefully, and you would have no time to wonder whether you are in a good or a bad mood.

I am telling you these things with all my affection, and I hope that you will understand them.

*

What is the method of increasing the "capacities of expansion and widening"?

I say there that a great variety of subjects should be studied. I believe that is it. For instance, if you are at school, to study all the subjects possible. If you are reading at home, not to read just one kind of thing, read all sorts of different things.

But, Sweet Mother, at school it is not possible to take many subjects. We have to specialise.

Yes, yes! I have heard that, especially from your teachers. I don't agree. And I know it very well, this is being continuously repeated to me: if anything is to be done properly, one must specialise. It is the same thing for sports also. It is the same for everything in life. It is said and repeated, and there are people who will prove it: to do something well one must specialise. One must do that and concentrate. If one wants to become a good philosopher, one must learn only philosophy, if one wants to be a good chemist, one must learn chemistry only. And if one wants to become a good tennis-player, one must play only tennis. That's not what I think, that is all I can say. My experience is different. I believe there are general faculties and that it is much more important to acquire these than to specialise – unless, naturally, it be like M and Mme Curie who wanted to develop a certain science, find something new, then of course, they were compelled to concentrate on that science. But still that was only till they had discovered it; once they had found it, nothing stopped them from widening their mind.

This is something I have heard from my very childhood, and I believe our great grand-parents heard the same thing, and from all time it has been preached that if you want to succeed in something you must do only that. And as for me, I was scolded all the time because I did many different things! And I was always told I would never be good at anything. I studied, I did painting, I did music, and besides was busy with other things still. And I was told my music wouldn't be up to much, my painting wouldn't be worthwhile, and my studies would be quite incomplete. Probably it is quite true, but still I have found that this had its advantages – those very advantages I am speaking about, of widening, making supple one's mind and understanding. It is true that if I had wanted to be a first-class player and to play in concerts, it would have been necessary to do what they said. And as for painting, if I had wanted to be among the great artists of the period, it would have been necessary to do that. That's quite understandable. But still, that is just one point of view. I don't see any necessity of being the greatest artist, the greatest musician. That has always seemed to me a vanity. And besides, it is a question of opinion....

There is but one instance, that's when one wants to make a discovery. Then, naturally, one must dedicate all one's effort to that. But that is not necessarily a whole lifetime's effort – unless one chooses a very difficult subject as the Curies did. There was a time they had made their discovery – they could go beyond it.

Yet spontaneously, people who wish to keep their balance rest from one activity and take up another. Examples are always cited of great performers or great artists or great scientists who have a kind of mania, a diversion. You have perhaps heard of Ingres's violin. Ingres was a painter; he did not lack talent and when he had some free time he started playing the violin, and his violin interested him much more than his painting. It seems he did not play the violin very well but it interested him more. And his painting he did very well and it interested him less. But I believe that was quite simply because he needed balance. Concentration on a single thing in order to attain one's aim is very necessary for the human mind in its normal functioning, but one can arrive at a different working that's more complete, more subtle. Naturally, physically one is bound to be limited, for in physical life one depends a great deal on time and space, and also it is difficult to realise great things without special concentration. But if one wants to lead a higher and deeper life, I believe one can acquire perhaps much greater capacities by other means than those of restriction and limitation. There is a considerable advantage in getting rid of one's limits, if not from the point of view of realisation in action, at least from that of spiritual realisation.

*

It is more important to pursue to its end the practice of the effect produced by an idea that one has met somehow, than to try to accumulate in the head a large number of ideas. Ideas may all be very useful in their own time, if they are allowed in at the opportune moment, particularly if you carry to the extreme limit the result of one of those dynamic ideas that are capable of making you win an inner victory. That is to say, one should have for one's chief, if not only aim the practice of what one knows rather than the accumulation in oneself of a knowledge which remains purely theoretical.

So one could sum up: put into practice integrally what you know, only then can you usefully increase your theoretical knowledge.

*

That is why you go to school, my children, whether you

are big or small, for one can learn at any age — and so you must go to your classes.

Sometimes, if you are not in a very good mood, you say, "How boring it is going to be!" Yes, perhaps the teacher who is taking your class does not know how to amuse you. He may be a very good teacher, but at the same time he may not know how to entertain you, for it is not always easy. There are days when one does not feel like being entertaining. There are days, for him as for you, when one would like to be elsewhere than in school. But still, you go to your class. You go because you must, for if you obey all your fancies you will never have any control over yourselves; your fancies will control you. So you go to your class, but instead of going there and thinking, "How bored I am going to be; I am sure it is not going to be interesting", you should tell yourselves, "There is not a single minute in life, not one circumstance that is not an opportunity for progress. So what progress am I going to make today? The class I am going to now is on a subject that does not interest me. But perhaps that is because something is lacking in me; perhaps, in my brain, a certain number of cells are deficient and that is why I cannot find any interest in the subject. If so, I shall try, I shall listen carefully, concentrate hard and above all drive out of my mind this aimlessness, this superficial shallowness which makes me feel bored when there is something I cannot grasp. I am bored because I do not make an effort to understand, because I do not have this will for progress." When one does not progress, one feels bored, everyone, young or old; for we are here on earth to progress. How tedious life would be without progress! Life is monotonous. Most often it is not fun. It is far from being beautiful. But if you take it as a field for progress, then everything changes, everything becomes interesting and there is no longer any room for boredom. Next time your teacher seems boring to you, instead of wasting your time doing nothing, try to understand why he bores you. Then if you have a capacity of observation and if you make an effort to understand, you will soon see that a kind of miracle has occurred and that you are no longer feeling bored at all.

This remedy is good in almost every case. Sometimes, in certain circumstances, everything seems dull, boring, stupid; this means that you are as boring as the circumstances and it clearly shows that you are not in a state of progress. It is simply a passing wave of boredom, and nothing is more contrary to the purpose of existence. At such a moment you might make an effort and ask yourself, "This boredom shows that I have something to learn, some progress to make in myself, some inertia to conquer, some weakness to overcome." Boredom is a dullness of the consciousness; and if you seek the cure within yourself, you will see that it immediately dissolves. Most people, when they feel bored, instead of making an effort to rise one step higher in their consciousness, come down one step lower; they come down even lower than they were before and do stupid things, they make themselves vulgar in the hope of amusing themselves. That is why men intoxicate themselves, spoil their health, deaden their brains. If they had risen instead of falling, they would have made use of this opportunity to progress.

*

The usefulness of work is nothing else but that: to crystallise this mental power. For, what you learn (unless you put it in practice by some work or deeper studies), half of what you learn, at least, will vanish, disappear with time. But it will leave behind one thing: the capacity of crystallising your thought, making something clear out of it, something precise, exact and organised. And that is the true usefulness of work: to organise your cerebral capacity. If you remain in your hazy movement in that kind of cloudy fluidity, you may labour for years, it will be quite useless to you; you will not come out of it more intelligent than when you entered it. But if you are able, even for half an hour, to concentrate your attention on things that seem to you of very little interest, like a rule of grammar, for example (the rules of grammar are some of the dry things I was speaking about, there are other things much more arid, but indeed the rules of grammar are sufficiently arid), if you take one of them and try to understand it – not learn it by heart and apply mechanically what you have learnt by heart, that will be of no use – but try to understand the thought behind the words: "Why was this rule formulated in this way?" and try to find out your own formula for the thing; that is so interesting. "Why has this gentleman who wrote this rule written it in this way? But I am studying, trying to understand why. Why has he put this word after that and that word after that other, and why has he stated the rule in this way? It is because he thought that it was the most complete and the most clear way of expressing the thing." And so that's the thing you must find. And when you find it, you suddenly exclaim: "That is what it means! It must be seen in this way, then it becomes very clear."

I am going to explain it to you: when you have understood, it forms a little crystal in you, like a little shining point. And when you have put in many, many, many of these, then you will begin to be intelligent. That is the utility of work, not simply to stuff the head with a heap of things that take you nowhere.

The Subjects of Study

Sri Aurobindo:

...There are two kinds of knowledge, that which seeks to understand the apparant phenomenon of existence externally, by an approach from outside, through the intellect, – this is the lower knowledge, the knowledge of the apparent world; secondly, the knowledge which seeks to know the truth of existence from within, in its source and reality, by spiritual realisation. Ordinarily, a sharp distinction is drawn between the two, and it is supposed that when we get to the higher knowledge, the God-knowledge, then the rest, the world-knowledge, becomes of no concern to us: but in reality they are two sides of one seeking. All knowledge is ultimately the knowledge of God, through himself, through Nature, through her works. Mankind has first to seek this knowledge through the external life; for until its mentality is sufficiently developed, spiritual knowledge is not really possible, and in proportion as it is developed, the possibilities of spiritual knowledge become richer and fuller.

Science, art, philosophy, ethics, psychology, the knowledge of man and his past, action itself are means by which we arrive at the knowledge of the workings of God through Nature and through life. At first it is the workings of life and forms of Nature which occupy us, but as we go deeper and deeper and get a completer view and experience, each of these lines brings us face to face with God. Science at its limits, even physical Science, is compelled to perceive in the end the infinite, the universal, the spirit, the divine intelligence and will in the

material universe. Still more easily must this be the end with
the psychic sciences which deal with the operations of higher
and subtler planes and powers of our being and come into contact with the beings and the phenomena of the worlds behind
which are unseen, not sensible by our physical organs, but
ascertainable by the subtle mind and senses. Art leads to the
same end; the aesthetic human being intensely preoccupied
with Nature through aesthetic emotion must in the end arrive
at spiritual emotion and perceive not only the infinite life, but
the infinite presence within her; preoccupied with beauty in
the life of man he must in the end come to see the divine, the
universal, the spiritual in humanity. Philosophy dealing with
the principles of things must come to perceive the Principle of
all these principles and investigate its nature, attributes and
essential workings. So ethics must eventually perceive that the
law of good which it seeks is the law of God and depends on
the being and nature of the Master of the law. Psychology leads
from the study of mind and the soul in living beings to the
perception of the one soul and one mind in all things and beings. The history and study of man like the history and study
of Nature leads towards the perception of the eternal and universal Power and Being whose thought and will work out
through the cosmic and human evolution. Action itself forces
us into contact with the divine Power which works through,
uses, overrules our actions. The intellect begins to perceive
and understand, the emotions to feel and desire and revere, the
will to turn itself to the service of the Divine without whom
Nature and man cannot exist or move and by conscious knowledge of whom alone we can arrive at our highest possibilities.

*

...all activities of knowledge that seek after or express Truth are in themselves rightful materials for a complete offering; none ought necessarily to be excluded from the wide framework of the divine life. The mental and physical sciences which examine into the laws and forms and processes of things, those which concern the life of men and animals, the social, political, linguistic and historical and those which seek to know and control the labours and activities by which man subdues and utilises his world and environment, and the noble and beautiful Arts which are at once work and knowledge, — for every well-made and significant poem, picture, statue or building is an act of creative knowledge, a living discovery of the consciousness, a figure of Truth, a dynamic form of mental and vital self-expression or world-expression, — all that seeks, all that finds, all that voices or figures is a realisation of something of the play of the Infinite and to that extent can be made a means of God-realisation or of divine formation. But the Yogin has to see that it is no longer done as part of an ignorant mental life; it can be accepted by him only if by the feeling, the remembrance, the dedication within it, it is turned into a movement of the spiritual consciousness and becomes a part of its vast grasp of comprehensive illuminating knowledge.

For all must be done as a sacrifice, all activities must have the One Divine for their object and the heart of their meaning. The Yogin's aim in the sciences that make for knowledge should be to discover and understand the workings of the Divine Consciousness-Puissance in man and creatures and things and forces, her creative significances, her execution of the mysteries, the symbols in which she arranges the manifestation. The Yogin's aim in the practical sciences, whether mental and physi-

cal or occult and psychic, should be to enter into the ways of
the Divine and his processes, to know the materials and means
for the work given to us so that we may use that knowledge for
a conscious and faultless expression of the spirit's mastery,
joy and self-fulfilment. The Yogin's aim in the Arts should not
be a mere aesthetic, mental or vital gratification, but, seeing
the Divine everywhere, worshipping it with a revelation of the
meaning of its works, to express that One Divine in gods and
men and creatures and objects.

*

At a certain stage of human development the aesthetic
sense is of infinite value in this direction. It raises and puri-
fies conduct by instilling a distaste for the coarse desires and
passions of the savage, for the rough, uncouth and excessive
in action and manner, and restraining both feeling and action
by a striving after the decent, the beautiful, the fit and seemly...

*

Art is subtle and delicate, and it makes the mind also in its
movements subtle and delicate. It is suggestive, and the intellect habituated to the appreciation of art is quick to catch
suggestions, mastering not only, as the scientific mind does,
that which is positive and on the surface, but that which leads
to ever fresh widening and subtilising of knowledge and opens
a door into the deeper secrets of inner nature where the positive instruments of science cannot take the depth or measure.
This supreme intellectual value of Art has never been sufficiently recognised.

*

Poetry raises the emotions and gives each its separate delight. Art stills the emotions and teaches them the delight of a restrained and limited satisfaction... Music deepens the emotions and harmonises them with each other. Between them music, art and poetry are a perfect education for the soul; they make and keep its movements purified, self-controlled, deep and harmonious. These, therefore, are agents which cannot profitably be neglected by humanity on its onward march or degraded to the mere satisfaction of sensuous pleasure which will disintegrate rather than build the character. They are, when properly used, great educating, edifying and civilising forces.

*

...The practice of imitation by the hand of the thing seen is of use both in detecting the lapses and inaccuracies of the mind, in noticing the objects of sense and in registering accurately what has been seen. Imitation by the hand ensures accuracy of observation. This is one of the first uses of drawing and it is sufficient in itself to make the teaching of this subject a necessary part of the training of the organs.

The Mother:
What are knowledge and intelligence? Have they important roles to play in our life?

Knowledge and intelligence are precisely the qualities of the higher mind in man which differentiate him from the animal.

Without knowledge and intelligence, one is not a man but an animal in human form.

*

To know how to read and write, to speak at least one language correctly, to know a little general geography, have an overall view of modern science and know some rules of conduct – this is indispensable for living in a group or a community.

*

The only really important thing modern science has discovered is that from the purely outer and physical point of view things are not what they seem to be. When you look at a body, a human being, an object, a landscape, you perceive these things with the help of your eyes, your touch, hearing and, for the details, smell and taste; well, science tells you: "All that is illusory, you don't see things at all as they are, you don't touch them as they really are, you don't smell them as they really are, you don't taste them as they really are. It is the structure of your organs which puts you in contact with these things in a particular way which is entirely superficial, external, illusory and unreal."

From the point of view of science, you are a mass of – not even of atoms – of something infinitely more imperceptible than an atom, which is in perpetual movement. There is absolutely nothing which is like a face, a nose, eyes, a mouth; it is only just an appearance. And scientists come to this conclusion – like the uncompromising spiritualists of the past – that the world is an illusion. That is a great discovery, very great.... One step more and they will enter into the Truth. So, when somebody comes and says, "But I *see* this, I *touch* it, I *feel* it, I am sure of it", from the scientific point of view it's nonsense. This could be said only by someone who has never made a scientific study of things as they are. So, by diametrically opposite roads they have come to the same result: the world as you see it is an illusion.

*

How can mathematics, history or science help me to find you?

They can help in several ways:
1. To become capable of receiving and bearing the light of the Truth, the mind must be made strong, wide and supple. These studies are a very good way to achieve this.
2. If you study science deeply enough, it will teach you the unreality of appearances and thus lead you to the spiritual reality.
3. The study of all the aspects and movements of physical Nature will bring you into contact with the universal Mother, and so you will be closer to me.

*

There are a lot of things that we need to know, not because we find them specially interesting but because they are useful and even indispensable; mathematics is one of them.

It is only when we have a strong background of knowledge that we can face life successfully.

*

History and geography can only become interesting to minds that are eager to know the earth on which they live.

Before one can take an interest in these two subjects, one must widen the horizons of one's thirst for knowledge as well as one's field of consciousness.

*

What is it we should look for in music?
How to judge the quality of a piece of music?
How to develop good taste (for music)?
What do you think of the light music (cinema, jazz, etc.)
which our children like very much?

The role of music lies in helping the consciousness to up-lift itself towards the spiritual heights.

All that lowers the consciousness, encourages desires and excites the passions runs counter to the true goal of music and ought to be avoided.

It is not a question of name but of inspiration – and the spiritual consciousness alone can be the judge there.

*

I don't know if any of you are so fond of music as to know how to hear it. But if you want to listen to music, you must create an absolute silence in your head, you must not follow or accept a single thought, and must be entirely concentrated, like a sort of screen which receives, without movement or noise, the vibration of the music. That is the only way, there is no other, the only way of hearing music and understanding it. If you admit in the least the movements and fancies of your thought, the whole value of the music escapes you.

*

Everyone should learn that. Especially everyone who

works here should learn that... not the Sanskrit of the scholars... all, all of them, wherever they may have been born....

Yes. Not Sanskrit from the point of view of scholarship, but Sanskrit, a Sanskrit — how to put it? — that opens the door to all the languages of India. I think that is indispensable. The ideal would be, in a few years, to have a rejuvenated Sanskrit as the representative language of India, that is, a Sanskrit spoken in such a way that — Sanskrit is behind all the languages of India and it should be that. This was Sri Aurobindo's idea, when we spoke about it.

Perfection of the Body

Sri Aurobindo:

...I would like to dwell for a while on the deeper raison d'être of such Associations and especially the need and utility for the nation of a widespread organisation of them and such sports or physical exercises as are practised here. In their more superficial aspect they appear merely as games and amusements which people take up for entertainment or as a field for the outlet of the body's energy and natural instinct of activity or for a means of the development and maintenance of the health and strength of the body; but they are or can be much more than that: they are also fields for the development of habits, capacities and qualities which are greatly needed and of the utmost service to a people in war or in peace, and in its political and social activities, in most indeed of the provinces of a combined human endeavour.

*

But of a higher import than the foundation, however necessary, of health, strength and fitness of the body is the development of discipline and morale and sound and strong character towards which these activities can help. There are many sports which are of the utmost value towards this end, because they help to form and even necessitate the qualities of courage, hardihood, energetic action and initiative or call for skill, steadiness of will or rapid decision and action, the perception of what is to be done in an emergency and dexterity in doing it. One development of the utmost value is the awakening of the essential instinctive body consciousness which can see and do what is necessary without any indication from mental thought and which is equivalent in the body to swift insight in the mind and spontaneous and rapid decision in the will. One may add the formation of a capacity for harmonious and right movements of the body, especially in a combined action, economic of physical effort and discouraging waste of energy, which result from such exercises as marches or drill and which displace the loose and straggling, the inharmonious or disorderly or wasteful movements common to the untrained individual body. Another invaluable result of these activities is the growth of what has been called the sporting spirit. That includes good humour and tolerance and consideration for all, a right attitude and friendliness to competitors and rivals, self-control and scrupulous observance of the laws of the game, fair play and avoidance of the use of foul means, an equal acceptance of victory or defeat without bad humour, resentment or ill-will towards successful competitors, loyal acceptance of the decisions of the appointed judge, umpire or referee. These qualities have their value for life in general and not only for sport, but the help that sport can give to their development is direct and invaluable.

The Mother:

We want to come in contact with the supreme consciousness, the universal consciousness, we want to bring it down in ourselves and to manifest it. But for that we must have a very solid base; our base is our physical being, our body. Therefore we have to build up a body solid, healthy, enduring, skilful, agile and strong, ready for everything. There is

no better way to prepare the body than physical exercise:
sports, athletics, gymnastics, and all games are the best means
to develop and strengthen the body.

*

So I invite you to participate in the programme beginning
today with enthusiasm and discipline – discipline, because it
is the imdispensable condition of order; enthusiasm, because
it is the essential condition of success.

*

That is why, as soon as the child is able to make use of his
limbs, some time should be devoted every day to the me-
thodical and regular development of all the parts of his body.
Every day some twenty or thirty minutes, preferably on waking, if possible, will be enough to ensure the proper functioning and balanced growth of his muscles while prevent-
ing any stiffening of the joints and of the spine, which occurs
much sooner than one thinks. In the general programme of
the child's education, sports and outdoor games should be
given a prominent place; that, more than all the medicines in
the world, will assure the child good health. An hour's mov-
ing about in the sun does more to cure weakness or even
anaemia than a whole arsenal of tonics. My advice is that
medicines should not be used unless it is absolutely impossible to avoid them; and this "absolutely impossible" should
be very strict. In this programme of physical culture, although
there are well-known general lines to be followed for the
best development of the human body, still, if the method is to
be fully effective in each case, it should be considered indi-

The Mother taking a French class for the children

The Mother with three little winners in the Playground

vidually, if possible with the help of a competent person, or
if not, by consulting the numerous manuals that have already
been and are still being published on the subject.

*

A physical culture which aims at building a body capable
of serving as a fit instrument for a higher consciousness demands very austere habits: a great regularity in sleep, food,
exercise and every activity. By a scrupulous study of one's
own bodily needs – for they very with each individual – a
general programme will be established; and once this has
been done well, it must be followed rigorously, without any
fantasy or slackness. There must be no little exceptions to
the rule that are indulged in "just for once" but which are
repeated very often – for as soon as one yields to temptation,
even "just for once", one lessens the resistance of the will-
power and opens the door to every failure. One must therefore forgo all weakness: no more nightly escapades from
which one comes back exhausted, no more feasting and ca-
rousing which upset the normal functioning of the stomach,
no more distractions, amusements and pleasures that only
waste energy and leave one without the strength to do the
daily practice. One must submit to the austerity of a sensible
and regular life, concentrating all one's physical attention on
building a body that comes as close to perfection as possible.

*

What is the difference between sports and physical education?

Sports are all the games, competitions, tournaments, etc., all the things based on contests and ending in placings and prizes.

Physical education means chiefly the combination of all exercises for the sake of the growth and upkeep of the body.

Naturally, here we have the two together. But it is particularly so because human beings, especially in their young age, still require some excitement in order to make an effort.

*

Mother, are sports competitions essential to our progress?

From the point of view of moral education they are rather essential, for if one can take part in them in the right spirit, it is a very good opportunity for mastering one's ego. If one does it without trying to overcome one's weaknesses and lower movements, one obviously doesn't know how to profit by them, and it does no good; but if one has the will to play in the right spirit, without any movement of a lower kind, without jealousy or ambition, keeping an attitude which could be called "fair play", that is, doing one's best and not caring about the result; if one can put in the utmost effort without being upset because one has not met with success or things have not turned out in one's favour, then it is very useful. One can come out of all these competitions with a greater self-control and a detachment from results which are a great help to the formation of an exceptional character. Naturally, if you do it in the ordinary way and with all the ordinary reactions and ugly movements, it doesn't help anything at all; but that holds good in no matter what one does; whether in the field of sports or the intellectual field, anywhere, if one acts in the ordinary way, one wastes one's time. But if when playing or taking part in tournaments and competitions, you keep the right spirit, it is a very good education, for it compels you to make a special effort and to exceed your ordinary limits a little. It is certainly an opportunity to make conscious many of your movements which otherwise would always remain unconscious.

*

Should one play in order to win?

When you have a three or four-year old consciousness, this is an altogether necessary stimulant. But you may have a four-year old consciousness even at the age of fifty, may you not? No, when you have a ripe consciousness you must not play in order to win. You must play for the sake of playing and to learn how to play and to progress in games and in order that your play may become the expression of your inner consciousness at its highest – it is this which is important. For example, people who like to play well do not go and choose bad players to play with, simply for the pleasure of winning – they choose those who are the best players and play with them. I remember having learnt to play tennis when I was eight, it was a passion; but I never wished to play with my little comrades because I learnt nothing (usually I used to defeat them), I always went to the best players. At times they looked surprised, but in the end they played with me – I never won but I learnt much.

*

I have seen that I am not able to force my physical body to do a little better than my actual capacity. I would like to know how I can force it. But, Sweet Mother, is it good to force one's body?

No.

The body is capable of progressing and it can gradually learn to do what it could not do before. But its capacity for progress is much slower than the vital desire for progress and the mental will for progress. And if the vital and the mind are left in charge of action, they simply harass the body, destroy its balance and upset its health.

Therefore, one must be patient and follow the rhythm of one's body, which is more reasonable and knows what it can and cannot do.

Naturally, some bodies are tamasic and need a little encouragement in order to progress.

But in all things and in all cases, one has to keep a balance.

Transformation of the Vital

The Mother:
   The vital being in us is the seat of impulses and desires, of enthusiasm and violence, of dynamic energy and desperate depressions, of passions and revolts. It can set everything in motion, build and realise; but it can also destroy and mar everything. Thus it may be the most difficult part to discipline in the human being. It is a long and exacting labour requiring great patience and perfect sincerity, for without sincerity you will deceive yourself from the very outset, and all endeavour for progress will be in vain. With the collaboration of the vital no realisation seems impossible, no transformation impracticable.... The vital is a good worker, but most often it seeks its own satisfaction. If that is refused, totally or even partially, the vital gets vexed, sulks and goes on strike. Its energy disappears more or less completely and in its place leaves disgust for people and things, discouragement or revolt, depression and dissatisfaction.

*

   All human beings are full of desires; their life is built by desires. The will of man is made of desire, his needs are desires. He can get rid of all these desires only by a constant vigilance and steady elimination.
   Each time that you feel excited or annoyed, each time that you are upset, you can be sure that there is a desire lurking behind the appearances.
   The sign of the true and Divine Consciousness is perfect

equality, constant equanimity and peace.

Excitement, irritation, sorrow, depression, upsetting belong all to the Physical Consciousness and must be sur-
mounted in order to get rid of the Falsehood.

*

There is another quality which must be cultivated in a child
from a very young age: that is the feeling of uneasiness, of a
moral disbalance which it feels when it has done certain things,
not because it has been told not to do them, not because it
fears punishment, but spontaneously. For example, a child
who hurts its comrade through mischief, if it is in its normal,
natural state, will experience uneasiness, a grief deep in its
being, because what it has done is contrary to its inner truth.

For in spite of all teachings, in spite of all that thought can
think, there is something in the depths which has a feeling of
a perfection, a greatness, a truth, and is painfully contradicted
by all the movements opposing this truth. If a child has not
been spoilt by its milieu, by deplorable examples around it,
that is, if it is in the normal state, spontaneously, without its
being told anything, it will feel an uneasiness when it has
done something against the truth of its being. And it is exactly
upon this that later its effort for progress must be founded.

*

When you acquire the habit of listening to this inner law,
when you obey it, follow it, try more and more to let it guide
your life, you create around you an atmosphere of truth and
peace and harmony which naturally reacts upon circumstances and forms, so to say, the atmosphere in which you

live. When you are a being of justice, truth, harmony, compassion, understanding, of perfect goodwill, this inner attitude, the more sincere and total it is, the more it reacts upon the external circumstances; not that it necessarily diminishes the difficulties of life, but it gives these difficulties a new meaning and that allows you to face them with a new strength and a new wisdom; whereas the man, the human being who follows his impulses, who obeys his desires, who has no time for scruples, who comes to live in complete cynicism, not caring for the effect that his life has upon others or for the more or less harmful consequences of his acts, creates for himself an atmosphere of ugliness, selfishness, conflict and bad will which necessarily acts more and more upon his consciousness and gives a bitterness to his life that in the end becomes a perpetual torment.

Of course this does not mean that such a man will not succeed in what he undertakes, that he will not be able to possess what he desires; these external advantages disappear only when there is within the inmost being a spark of sincerity which persists and makes him worthy of this misfortune.

If you see a bad man become unlucky and miserable, you must immediately respect him. It means that the flame of inner sincerity is not altogether extinguished and something still reacts to his bad actions.

*

How can one transform the vital?

The first step: will. Secondly, sincerity and aspiration. But will and aspiration are almost the same thing, one follows the other. Then, perseverance. Yes, perseverance is necessary in any process, and what is this process?... First, there must be the ability to observe and discern, the ability to find the vital in oneself, else you will be hard put to it to say: "This comes from the vital, this comes from the mind, this from the body." Everything will seem to you mixed and indistinct.

After a very sustained observation, you will be able to distinguish between the different parts and recognise the origin of a movement. Quite a long time is necessary for this, but one can go quite fast also, it depends upon people. But once you have found out the different parts ask yourself, "What is there of the vital in this? What does the vital bring into your consciousness? In what way does it change your movements; what does it add to them and what take away? What happens in your consciousness through the intervention of the vital?" Once you know this, what do you do?... Then you will need to watch this intervention, observe it, find out in what way it works. For instance, you want to transform your vital. You have a great sincerity in your aspiration and the resolution to go to the very end. You have all that. You start observing and you see that two things can happen (many things can happen) but mainly two.

First, a sort of enthusiasm takes hold of you. You set to work earnestly. In this enthusiasm you think, "I am going to do this and that, I am going to reach my goal immediately, everything is going to be magnificent! It will see, this vital, how I am going to treat it if it doesn't obey!" And if you look carefully you will see that the vital is saying to itself, "Ah, at last, here's an opportunity!" It accepts, it starts working with all its zeal, all its enthusiasm and... all its impatience.

The second thing may be the very opposite. A sort of un-easiness: "I am not well, how tedious life is, how wearisome everything. How am I going to do all that? Will I ever reach the goal? Is it worth while beginning? Is it at all possible? Isn't it impossible?" It is the vital which is not very happy about what is going to be done for it, which does not want anyone to meddle in its affairs, which does not like all that very much. So it suggests depression, discouragement, a lack of faith, doubt – is it really worth the trouble?

These are the two extremes, and each has its difficulties, its obstacles.

Depression, unless one has a strong will, suggests, "This is not worth while, one may have to wait a lifetime." Enthu-siasm, it expects to see the vital transformed overnight: "I am not going to have any difficulty henceforth, I am going to advance rapidly on the path of yoga, I am going to gain the divine consciousness without any difficulty." There are some other difficulties.... One needs a little time, much persever-ance. So the vital, after a few hours – perhaps a few days, perhaps a few months – says to itself: "We haven't gone very far with our enthusiasm, has anything been really done? Doesn't this movement leave us just where we were? – per-haps worse than we were, a little troubled, a little disturbed? Things are no longer what they were, they are not yet what they ought to be. It is very tiresome, what I am doing." And then, if one pushes a little more, here's this gentleman say-ing, "Ah! no, I have had enough of it, leave me alone. I don't want to move, I shall stay in my corner, I won't trouble you, but don't bother me!" And so one has not gone very much farther than before.

This is one of the big obstacles which must be carefully avoided. As soon as there is the least sign of discontentment, of annoyance, the vital must be spoken to in this way, "My friend, you are going to keep calm, you are going to do what you are asked to do, otherwise you will have to deal with me." And to the other, the enthusiast who says, "Everything must be done now, immediately", your reply is, "Calm yourself a little, your energy is excellent, but it must not be spent in five minutes. We shall need it for a long time, keep it carefully and, as it is wanted, I shall call upon your goodwill. You will show that you are full of goodwill, you will obey, you won't grumble, you will not protest, you will not revolt, you will say 'yes, yes.' You will make a little sacrifice when asked, you will say 'yes' whole-heartedly."

So we get started on the path. But the road is very long. Many things happen on the way. Suddenly one thinks one has overcome an obstacle; I say "thinks", because though one has overcome it, it is not totally overcome. I am going to take a very obvious instance, of a very simple observation. Someone has found that his vital is uncontrollable and uncontrolled, that it gets furious for nothing and about nothing. He starts working to teach it not to get carried away, not to flare up, to remain calm and bear the shocks of life without reacting violently. If one does this cheerfully, it goes quite quickly (note this well, it is very important: when you have to deal with your vital take care to keep your good humour, otherwise you will get into trouble). One keeps one's good humour, that is, when one sees the fury rise, one begins to laugh. Instead of being depressed and saying, "Ah! in spite of all my effort it is beginning all over again", one begins to laugh and says, "Well, well! one hasn't yet seen the end of it. Look now, aren't you ridiculous, you know quite well that you are being ridiculous! Is it worthwhile getting angry?" One gives it this lesson good-humouredly. And really, after a while it doesn't get angry again, it is quiet – and one relaxes one's attention. One thinks the difficulty has been overcome, one thinks a result has at last been reached: "My vital does not trouble me any longer, it does not get angry now, everything is going fine." And the next day, one loses one's temper. It is then one must be careful, it is then one must not say, "Here we are, it's no use, I shall never achieve anything, all my efforts are futile; all this is an illusion, it is impossible." On the contrary, one must say, "I wasn't vigilant enough." One must wait long, very long, before one can say, "Ah! it is done and finished." Sometimes one must wait for years, many years....

You must arm yourself with an endless patience and endurance. You do a thing once, ten times, a hundred times, a thousand times if necessary, but you do it till it gets done. And not done only here and there, but everywhere and everywhere at the same time. This is the great problem one sets oneself.

*

How can the senses be used for self-development?

Developing through sensations? It is very much in fashion. It is much in fashion. Now in the schools certain disciplines are invented to develop children's power of observation, the quickness of decision, of choice, the capacity to reckon with the eyes, appreciation, all that. All kinds of games are made for children now, to teach them all that. The sense of hearing can also be developed, the sense of smell, the sense of sight – all these can be methodically developed. If, instead of merely living in one's sensations - this is "pleasant or unpleasant", this is "pleasing or displeasing" and all kinds of things which are perfectly useless – one succeeds in calculating, measuring, comparing, noting, studying in detail all the vibrations.... You see, human beings live like blind men, constantly, absolutely unconscious, and they plunge into sensations and reactions, all the impulses, and so it is pleasant, it is unpleasant, it is pleasing, it is displeasing, all that. What is all that, then? What's the sense in it? – None at all. One ought to be able to appreciate, calculate, judge, compare, note, know exactly and scientifically the full value of the vibrations, the relations between things, study everything, everything – for instance, study all sensations in connection with the reactions they produce, follow the movement from the sensation to the brain, and then follow the movement of response from the brain to the sensations. And in this way one succeeds in controlling one's will, one's sensations completely, to such an extent that if there is something one does not want to feel, it is enough, with one's will, to cut it off: one feels it no longer. There are many disciplines of this kind. Some of them keep you busy for a lifetime, and if they are well followed, you don't waste a moment and are altogether interested. You no longer have time for impulses, this takes away all impulses. When you become scientific in these studies, you are no longer like a cork: one wave sending you here, another sending you there! There is a passing movement of Nature. Nature, oh how she plays with men! Good heavens, when you see how it is, oh! truly it is enough to make you revolt. I don't understand how they do not revolt.... She sends round a wave of desire, and they are all like sheep running after their desires; she sends round a wave of violence, they are once again like other sheep living in violence, and so on, for everything. Anger – she just does "poof", and everybody gets into a rage. She has but to make a gesture – a gesture of her caprice – and the human mobs follow. Or else it passes from one to another, just like that; they don't know why. They are asked, "Why?" – "Well, suddenly I felt angry. Suddenly I was seized by desire." Oh! it is shameful.

Development of the Mind

Sri Aurobindo:

How can one develop the intellect?

By training it to see, observe, understand in the right way. Reading and study are only useful to acquire information and widen one's field of data. But that comes to nothing if one does not know how to discern and discriminate, judge, see what is within and behind things.

*

What you can do is to read not for pastime but with the clear intention of furnishing your mind with knowledge.

*

Study is of importance only if you study in the right way and with the turn for knowledge and mental discipline.

*

A man may have read much and yet be mentally undeveloped. It is by thinking, understanding, receiving mental influences from his intellectual superiors that a man's mind develops.

The Mother:

It is a good thing to begin to learn at an early age that to lead an efficient life and obtain from one's body the maximum it is able to give, reason must be the master of the house.

And it is not a question of yoga or higher realisation, it is
something which should be taught everywhere, in every
school, every family, every home: man was made to be a mental
being, and merely to be a man – we are not speaking of anything else, we are speaking only of being a man – life must be
dominated by reason and not by vital impulses. This should
be taught to all children from their infancy. If one is not dominated by reason, one is a brute lower than the animal; for
animals don't have a mind or a reason to dominate them, but
they obey the instinct of the species. There is an instinct of the
species which is an extremely reasonable instinct that regu-
lates all their activities for their own good, and automatically,
without knowing it, they are subject to this instinct of the
species which is altogether reasonable from the point of view
of that species, of each species.... Stupidities and perversion
begin with conscious mind and the human species. It is the
wrong use man makes of his mental capacity. Perversion
begins with humanity. It is a distortion of the progress of Nature
which mental consciousness represents. And, therefore, the
first thing which should be taught to every human being as
soon as he is able to think, is that he should obey reason which
is a super-instinct of the species. Reason is the master of the
nature of mankind. One must obey reason and absolutely refuse
to be the slave of instincts. And here I am not talking to you
about yoga, I am not talking about spiritual life, not at all; it
has nothing to do with that. It is the basic wisdom of human
life, purely human life: every human being who obeys anything other than reason is a kind of brute lower than the animal. That's all. And this should be taught everywhere; it is the
basic education which should be given to children.

The reign of reason must come to an end only with the advent of the psychic law which manifests the divine Will.

*

To complement this movement of inner discovery, it would be good not to neglect the development of the mind. For the mental instrument can equally be a great help or a great hindrance. In its natural state the human mind is always limited in its vision, narrow in its understanding, rigid in its conceptions, and a constant effort is therefore needed to widen it, to make it more supple and profound. So it is very necessary to consider everything from as many points of view as possible. Towards this end, there is an exercise which gives great suppleness and elevation to the thought. It is as follows: a clearly formulated thesis is set; against it is opposed its antithesis, formulated with the same precision. Then by careful reflection the problem must be widened or transcended until a synthesis is found which unites the two contraries in a larger, higher and more comprehensive idea.

Many other exercises of the same kind can be undertaken; some have a beneficial effect on the character and so possess a double advantage: that of educating the mind and that of establishing control over the feelings and their consequences. For example, you must never allow your mind to judge things and people, for the mind is not an instrument of knowledge; it is incapable of finding knowledge, but it must be moved by knowledge. Knowledge belongs to a much higher domain than that of the human mind, far above the region of pure ideas. The mind has to be silent and attentive to receive knowledge from above and manifest it. For it is an instrument of formation, of organisation and action, and it is in these functions that it attains its full value and real usefulness.

There is another practice which can be very helpful to the progress of the consciousness. Whenever there is a disagreement on any matter, such as a decision to be taken, or an action to be carried out, one must never remain closed up in one's own conception or point of view. On the contrary, one must make an effort to understand the other's point of view, to put oneself in his place and, instead of quarrelling or even fighting, find the solution which can reasonably satisfy both parties; there always is one for men of goodwill.

*

...The human mind is a public place open on all sides, and in this public place, things come, go, cross from all directions; and some settle there and these are not always the best. And there, to obtain control over that multitude is the most difficult of all controls. Try to control the thought coming into your mind, you will see. Simply, you will see to what a degree you have to be watchful, like a sentinel, with the eyes of the mind wide open, and then keep an extremely clear vision of the ideas which conform to your aspirations and those which do not. And you must police at every minute that public place where roads from all sides meet, so that all passers-by do not rush in. It is a big job. Then, don't forget that even if you make sincere efforts, it is not in a day, not in a month, not in a year that you will reach the end of all these difficulties. When one begins, one must begin with an unshakable patience. One must say, "Even if it takes fifty years, even if it takes a hundred years, even if it takes several lives, what I want to accomplish, I shall accomplish."

*

However that may be, I believe it is a practice to be rec-
ommended to everyone: to keep a certain time every day for
trying to make the mind quiet, even, still. And it is an unde-
niable fact that the more mentally developed one is, the
quicker one succeeds; and the more the mind is in a rudi-
mentary state, the more difficult it is.

Those who are at the bottom of the scale, who have never
trained their minds, find it necessary to speak in order to
think. It happens even that it is the sound of their voice which
enables them to associate ideas; if they do not express them,
they do not think. At a higher level there are those who still
have to move words about in their heads in order to think,
even though they do not utter them aloud. Those who truly
begin to think are those who are able to think without words,
that is to say, to be in contact with the idea and express it
through a wide variety of words and phrases. There are higher
degrees – many higher degrees – but those who think without words truly begin to reach an intellectual state and for
them it is much easier to make the mind quiet, that is to say,
to stop the movement of associating the words that constantly
move about like passers-by in a public square, and to con-
template an idea in silence.

I emphasise this fact because there are quite a few people
who, when mental silence has been transmitted to them by
occult means, are immediately alarmed and afraid of losing
their intelligence. Because they can no longer think, they fear
they may become stupid! But to cease thinking is a much

higher achievement than to be able to spin out thoughts end-
lessly and it demands a much greater development.

So from every point of view, and not only from the spiritual point of view, it is always very good to practise silence
for a few minutes, at least twice a day, but it must be a true
silence, not merely abstention from talking.

Psychic Education

The Mother:

We give the name "psychic" to the psychological centre of our being, the seat within us of the highest truth of our existence, that which can know this truth and set it in movement. It is therefore of capital importance to become conscious of its presence in us, to concentrate on this presence until it becomes a living fact for us and we can identify ourselves with it.

In various times and places many methods have been prescribed for attaining this perception and ultimately achieving this identification. Some methods are psychological, some religious, some even mechanical. In reality, everyone has to find the one which suits him best, and if one has an ardent and steadfast aspiration, a persistent and dynamic will, one is sure to meet, in one way or another – outwardly through reading and study, inwardly through concentration, meditation, revelation and experience – the help one needs to reach the goal. Only one thing is absolutely indispensable: the will to discover and to realise. This discovery and realisation should be the primary preoccupation of our being, the pearl of great price which we must acquire at any cost. Whatever you do, whatever your occupations and activities, the will to find the truth of your being and to unite with it must be always living and present behind all that you do, all that you feel, all that you think.

*

Every human being carries hidden within him the possibility of a greater consciousness which goes beyond the bounds of his present life and enables him to share in a higher and a vaster life. Indeed, in all exceptional beings it is always this consciousness that governs their lives and organises both the circumstances of their existence and their individual reaction to these circumstances. What the human mental consciousness does not know and cannot do, this consciousness knows and does. It is like a light that shines at the centre of the being, radiating through the thick coverings of the external consciousness.

*

It is through this psychic presence that the truth of an individual being comes into contact with him and the circumstances of his life. In most cases the presence acts, so to say, from behind the veil, unrecognised and unknown; but in some, it is perceptible and its action recognisable and even, in a very few, the presence becomes tangible and its action fully effective. These go forward in life with an assurance and a certitude all their own; they are masters of their destiny. It is for the purpose of obtaining this mastery and becoming conscious of the psychic presence that psychic education should be practised. But for that there is need of a special factor, the personal will. For till now, the discovery of the psychic being and identification with it have not been among the recognised subjects of education, and although one can find in special treatises useful and practical hints on the subject, and although in exceptional cases one may have the good fortune of meeting someone who is capable of showing the way and giving the help that is needed to follow it, most often the attempt is left to one's own personal initiative. The discovery is a personal matter and a great determination, a strong will and an untiring perseverance are indispensable to reach the goal. Each one must, so to say, trace out his own path through his own difficulties. The goal is known to some extent, for most of those who have reached it have described it more or less clearly. But the supreme value of the discovery lies in its spontaneity, its ingenuousness, and that escapes all ordinary mental laws. And that is why anyone wanting to take up the adventure usually first seeks out some person who has successfully undertaken it and is able to sustain him and enlighten him on his way. Yet there are some solitary travellers and for them a few general indications may be useful.

The starting-point is to seek in yourself that which is independent of the body and the circumstances of life, which is not born of the mental formation that you have been given, the language you speak, the habits and customs of the environment in which you live, the country where you are born or the age to which you belong. You must find, in the depths of your being, that which carries in it a sense of universality, limitless expansion, unbroken continuity. Then you decentralise, extend and widen yourself; you begin to live in all things and in all beings; the barriers separating individuals from each other break down. You think in their thoughts, vibrate in their sensations, feel in their feelings, live in the life of all. what seemed inert suddenly becomes full of life, stones quicken, plants feel and will and suffer, animals speak in a language more or less inarticulate, but clear and expressive; everything is animated by a marvellous consciousness without time or limit. And this is only one aspect of the psychic realisation; there are others, many others. All help you to go beyond the barriers of your egoism, the walls of your external personality, the impotence of your reactions and the incapacity of your will.

*

You wrote to me that it is not easy to come in contact with the psychic being. Why do You consider it difficult? How should I begin?

I said "not easy", because the contact is not spontaneous – it is involuntary. The psychic being always has an influence on the thoughts and actions, but one is rarely conscious of it. To become conscious of the psychic being, one must want to do so, make one's mind as silent as possible, and enter deep into the heart of one's being, beyond sensations and thoughts. One must form the habit of silent concentration and descent into the depths of one's being.

The discovery of the psychic being is a definite and very concrete fact, as all who have had the experience know.

Power of Concentration

The Mother:

...whatever you may want to do in life, one thing is absolutely indispensable and at the basis of *everything*, the capacity of concentrating the attention. If you are able to gather together the rays of attention and consciousness on one point and can maintain this concentration with a persistent will, *nothing* can resist it – whatever it may be, from the most material physical development to the highest spiritual one. But this discipline must be followed in a constant and, it may be said, imperturbable way; not that you should always be concentrated on the same thing – that's not what I mean, I mean learning to concentrate.

And materially, for studies, sports, all physical or mental development, it is absolutely indispensable. And the value of an individual is proportionate to the value of his attention.

And from the spiritual point of view it is still more important. There is *no* spiritual obstacle which can resist a penetrating power of concentration. For instance, the discovery of the psychic being, union with the inner Divine, opening to the higher spheres, *all* can be obtained by an intense and obstinate power of concentration – but one must learn how to do it.

There is nothing in the human or even in the superhuman field, to which the power of concentration is not the key.

You can be the best athlete, you can be the best student, you can be an artistic, literary or scientific genius, you can be the greatest saint with that faculty. And everyone has in himself a tiny little beginning of it – it is given to everybody, but people do not cultivate it.

*

What is concentration?

It is to bring back all the scattered threads of consciousness to a single point, a single idea. Those who can attain perfect attention succeed in everything they undertake; they will always make a rapid progress. And this kind of concentration can be developed exactly like the muscles; one may follow different systems, different methods of training. Today we know that the most pitiful weakling, for example, can with discipline become as strong as anyone else. One should not have a will which flickers out like a candle.

The will, concentration must be cultivated; it is a question of method, of regular exercise. If you will, you can.

But the thought "What's the use?" must not come in to weaken the will. The idea that one is born with a certain character and can do nothing about it is a stupidity.

*

When one works and wants to do one's best, one needs much time. But generally we don't have much time, we are in a hurry. How to do one's best when one is in a hurry?

It is a very interesting subject and I wanted to speak to you about it in detail, one day. Generally when men are in a hurry, they do not do completely what they have to do or they do badly what they do. Well, there is a third way, it is to

intensify one's concentration. If you do that you can gain
half the time, even from a very short time. Take a very ordinary example: to have your bath and to dress; the time needed
varies with people, doesn't it? but let us say, half an hour is
required for doing everything without losing time and without hurrying. Then, if you are in a hurry, one of two things
happens: you don't wash so well or you dress badly! But
there is another way – to concentrate one's attention and one's
energy, think only of what one is doing and not of anything
else, not to make a movement too much, to make the exact
movement in the most exact way, and (it is an experience
lived, I can speak of it with certitude) you can do in fifteen
minutes what you were formerly doing in half an hour, and
do it as well, at times even better, without forgetting anything, without leaving out anything, simply by the intensity
of the concentration.

*

What are the causes for not being able to meditate?

Because one has not learnt to do it.

Why, suddenly you take a fancy: today I am going to meditate. You have never done so before. You sit down and imagine you are going to begin meditating. But it is something to
learn as one learns mathematics or the piano. It is not learnt
just like that! It is not enough to sit with crossed arms and
crossed legs in order to meditate. You must learn how to
meditate. Everywhere all kinds of rules have been given about
what should be done in order to be able to meditate.

If, when one was quite young and was taught, for instance,

how to squat, if one was taught at the same time not to think or to remain very quiet or to concentrate or gather one's thoughts, or... all sorts of things one must learn to do, like meditating; if, when quite young and at the same time that you were taught to stand straight, for instance, and walk or sit or even eat – you are taught many things but you are not aware of this, for they are taught when you are very small – if you were taught to meditate also, then spontaneously, later, you could, the day you decide to do so, sit down and meditate. But you are not taught this. You are taught absolutely nothing of the kind. Besides, usually you are taught very few things – you are not taught even to sleep. People think that they have only to lie down in their bed and then they sleep. But this is not true! One must learn how to sleep as one must learn to eat, learn to do anything at all. And if one does not learn, well, one does it badly! Or one takes years and years to learn how to do it, and during all those years when it is badly done, all sorts of unpleasant things occur. And it is only after suffering much, making many mistakes, committing many stupidities, that, gradually, when one is old and has white hair, one begins to know how to do something. But if, when you were quite small, your parents or those who look after you, took the trouble to teach you how to do what you do, do it properly as it should be done, in the right way, then that would help you to avoid all – all these mistakes you make through the years. And not only do you make mistakes, but nobody tells you they are mistakes! And so you are surprised that you fall ill, are tired, don't know how to do what you want to, and that you have never been taught. Some children are not taught anything, and so they need years and years and years to learn the simplest things, even the most elementary thing: to be clean.

It is true that most of the time parents do not teach this because they do not know it themselves! For they themselves did not have anyone to teach them. So they do not know... they have groped in the dark all their life to learn how to live. And so naturally they are not in a position to teach you how to live, for they do not know it themselves. If you are left to yourself, you understand, it needs years, years of experience to learn the simplest thing, and even then you must think about it. If you don't think about it, you will never learn.

To live in the right way is a very difficult art, and unless one begins to learn it when quite young and to make an effort, one never knows it very well. Simply the art of keeping one's body in good health, one's mind quiet and goodwill in one's heart – things which are indispensable in order to live decently – I don't say in comfort, I don't say remarkably, I only say decently. Well, I don't think there are many who take care to teach this to their children.

Importance of Work

The Mother:

In work too there is an austerity. It consists in not having any preferences and in doing everything one does with interest. For one who wants to grow in self-perfection, there are no great or small tasks, none that are important or unimportant; all are equally useful for one who aspires for progress and self-mastery. It is said that one only does well what one is interested in doing. This is true, but it is truer still that one can learn to find interest in everything one does, even in what appear to be the most insignificant chores. The secret of this attainment lies in the urge towards self-perfection. Whatever occupation or task falls to your lot, you must do it with a will to progress; whatever one does, one must not only do it as best one can but strive to do it better and better in a constant effort for perfection. In this way everything without exception becomes interesting, from the most material chore to the most artistic and intellectual work. The scope for progress in infinite and can be applied to the smallest thing.

*

Truly speaking, it depends more on the way of doing a thing than on the thing itself.

You take up some work which is quite material, like cleaning the floor or dusting a room; well, it seems to me that this work can lead to a very deep consciousness if it is done with a certain feeling for perfection and progress; while other work considered of a higher kind as, for example, studies or liter-

ary and artistic work, if done with the idea of seeking fame
or for the satisfaction of one's vanity or for some material
gain, will not help you to progress. So this is already a kind
of classification which depends more on the inner attitude
than on the outer fact. But this classification can be applied
to everything.

*

How are we to know, you will ask, when it is the Divine
Will that makes us act? The Divine Will is not difficult to
recognise. It is unmistakable. You can know it without being
very far on the path. Only you must listen to its voice, the
small voice that is here in the heart. Once you are accustomed to listen, if you do anything that is contrary to the
Divine Will, you feel an uneasiness. If you persist on the
wrong track, you get very much disturbed. If, however, you
give some material excuse as the cause of your uneasiness
and proceed on your way, you gradually lose the faculty of
perception and finally you may go on doing all kinds of wrong
and feel no uneasiness. But if, when once you feel the least
disturbance, you stop and ask of your inner self, "What is the
cause of this?" then you do get the real answer and the whole
thing becomes quite clear. Do not try to give a material excuse when you feel a little depression or a slight uneasiness.

*

...if you want to do something well, whatever it may be,
any kind of work, the least thing, play a game, write a book,
do painting or music or run a race, anything at all, if you
want to do it well, you must *become* what you are doing and

not remain a small person looking at himself doing it; for if one looks at oneself acting, one is... one is still in complicity with the ego. If, in oneself, one succeeds in becoming what one does, it is a great progress. In the least little details, one must learn this. Take a very amusing instance: you want to fill a bottle from another bottle; you concentrate (you may try it as a discipline, as a gymnastic); well, as long as you are the bottle to be filled, the bottle from which one pours, and the movement of pouring, as long as you are only this, all goes well. But if unfortunately you think at a given moment: "Ah! it is getting on well, I am managing well", the next minute it spills over! It is the same for everything, for everything. That is why work is a good means of discipline, for if you want to do the work properly, you must *become* the work instead of being someone who works , otherwise you will never do it well. If you remain "someone who works" and, besides, if your thoughts go vagabonding, then you may be sure that if you are handling fragile things they will break, if you are cooking, you will burn something, or if you are playing a game, you will miss all the balls! It is here, in this, that work is a great discipline. For if truly you want to do it well, this is the only way of doing it.

There we are. When you are at school, you must become the concentration which tries to catch what the teacher is saying, or the thought which enters you or the knowledge you are given. That is what you must be. You must not think of yourself but only of what you want to learn. And you will see that your capacities will immediately be doubled.

*

Would it not be better to continue the work even if one feels lazy?

That depends on the work; there we enter another domain. If it is a work that you are doing for the collectivity and not for yourself personally, then you must do it, whatever happens. It is an elementary discipline. You have undertaken to do this work or have been given the work and have taken it up, therefore you have accepted it, and in that case you must do it. At all times, unless you are absolutely ill, ill in the last degree and unable to move, you must do it. Even if you are rather ill, you must do it. An unselfish work always cures you of your petty personal maladies. Naturally, if you are really compelled to be in bed without being able to move, with a terrible fever or a very serious illness, then that's quite different. But otherwise, if you are just a little indisposed: "I am not feeling quite well, I have a little headache or I have indigestion, or I have a bad cold, I am coughing", things like that – then doing your work, not thinking of yourself, thinking of the work, doing it as well as you can, that puts you right immediately.

How to Sleep

The Mother:

It does not consist in going without sleep but in knowing how to sleep. Sleep must not be a fall into unconsciousness which makes the body heavy instead of refreshing it. Eating with moderation and abstaining from all excess greatly reduces the need to spend many hours in sleep; however, the quality of sleep is much more important than its quantity. In order to have a truly effective rest and relaxation during sleep, it is good as a rule to drink something before going to bed, a cup of milk or soup or fruit-juice, for instance. Light food brings a quiet sleep. One should, however, abstain from all copious meals, for then the sleep becomes agitated and is disturbed by nightmares, or else is dense, heavy and dulling. But the most important thing of all is to make the mind clear, to quieten the emotions and calm the effervescence of desires and the preoccupations which accompany them. If before retiring to bed one has talked a lot or had a lively discussion, if one has read an exciting or intensely interesting book, one should rest a little without sleeping in order to quieten the mental activity, so that the brain does not engage in disorderly movements while the other parts of the body alone are asleep. Those who practise meditation will do well to concentrate for a few minutes on a lofty and restful idea, in an aspiration towards a higher and vaster consciousness. Their sleep will benefit greatly from this and they will largely be spared the risk of falling into unconsciousness while they sleep.

*

How is it better to go to bed early and to get up early?

When the sun sets, a kind of peace descends upon the earth and this peace is helpful for sleep.

When the sun rises, a vigorous energy descends upon the earth and this energy is helpful for work.

When you go to bed late and get up late, you contradict the forces of Nature and that is not very wise.

*

There is no end to the discoveries that you can make in dreams. But one thing is very important: never go to sleep when you are very tired, for if you do, you fall into a sort of unconsciousness and dreams do with you whatever they like, without your being able to exercise the least control. Just as you should always rest before eating, I would advise you all to rest before going to sleep. But then you must know how to rest.

There are many ways of doing it. Here is one: first of all, put your body at ease, comfortably stretched out on a bed or in an easy-chair. Then try to relax your nerves, all together or one by one, till you have obtained complete relaxation. This done, and while your body lies limp like a rag on the bed, make your brain silent and immobile, till it is no longer conscious of itself. Then slowly, imperceptibly, pass from this state into sleep. When you wake up the next morning, you will be full of energy. On the contrary, if you go to bed completely tired and without relaxing yourself, you will fall into a heavy, dull and unconscious sleep in which the vital will lose all its energies.

It is possible that you may not obtain an immediate result, but persevere.

*

At times I talk in my sleep. It is a sign that the mind lacks control, isn't it? So what should I do to keep it quiet at night?

Generally when the body is asleep at night, the mind goes out because it is difficult for it to remain quiet for a long time; and that is why most people do not talk.

But your mind seems to remain in your body, so you must ask it to remain perfectly quiet and silent so that your body can rest properly. A little concentration for that, before going to sleep, will surely be effective.

*

We must therefore learn to know our dreams, and first of all to distinguish between them, for they are very varied in nature and quality....

As a general rule, each individual has a period of the night that is more favourable for dreams, during which his activity is more fertile, more intellectual, and the mental circumstances of the environment in which he moves are more interesting.

The great majority of dreams have no other value than that of a purely mechanical and uncontrolled activity of the physical brain, in which certain cells continue to function during sleep as generators of sensory images and impressions conforming to the pictures received from outside.

These dreams are nearly always caused by purely physical circumstances — state of health, digestion, position in bed, etc.

With a little self-obervation and a few precautions, it is easy to avoid this type of dream, which is as useless as it is tiring, by eliminating its physical causes.

There are also other dreams which are nothing but futile manifestations of the erratic activities of certain mental faculties, which associate ideas, conversations and memories that come together at random.

Such dreams are already more significant, for these erratic activities reveal to us the confusion that prevails in our mental being as soon as it is no longer subject to the control of our will, and show us that this being is still not organised or ordered within us, that it is not mature enough to have an autonomous life.

Almost the same in form to these, but more important in their consequences, are the dreams which I mentioned just now, those which arise from the inner being seeking revenge when it is freed for a moment from the constraint that we impose upon it. These dreams often enable us to perceive tendencies, inclinations, impulses, desires of which we were not conscious so long as our will to realise our ideal kept them concealed in some obscure recess of our being.

*

However, as an initial help to set you on the path, I can tell you: (1) that on getting up, before starting the day, it is good to make an offering of this day to the Divine, an offering of all that one thinks, all that one is, all that one will do; (2) and at night, before going to sleep, it is good to review

the day, taking note of all the times one has forgotten or neglected to make an offering of one's self or one's action, and
to aspire or pray that these lapses do not recur.

This is a minimum, a very small beginning – and it should
increase with the sincerity of your consecration.

Attitude towards Food

Sri Aurobindo:

Too much eating makes the body material and heavy, eating too little makes it weak and nervous – one has to find the true harmony and balance between the body's need and the food taken.

*

It is the attachment to food, the greed and eagerness for it, making it an unduly important thing in the life, that is contrary to the spirit of yoga. To be aware that something is pleasant to the palate is not wrong; only one must have no desire nor hankering for it, no exultation in getting it, no displeasure or regret at not getting it. One must be calm and equal, not getting upset or dissatisfied when the food is not tasty or not in abundance – eating the fixed amount that is necessary, not less or more. There should be neither eagerness nor repugnance.

To be always thinking about food and troubling the mind is quite the wrong way of getting rid of the food-desire. Put the food element in the right place in the life, in a small corner, and don't concentrate on it but on other things.

*

The Mother:

The body in its normal state, that is to say, when there is no intervention of mental notions or vital impulses, also knows very well what is good and necessary for it; but for this to be effective in practice, one must educate the child with care and teach him to distinguish his desires from his needs. He should be helped to develop a taste for food that is simple and healthy, substantial and appetising, but free from any useless complications. In his daily food, all that merely stuffs and causes heaviness shuld be avoided; and above all, he must be taught to eat according to his hunger, neither more nor less, and not to make his meals an occasion to satisfy his greed or gluttony. From one's very childhood, one should know that one eats in order to give strength and health to the body and not to enjoy the pleasures of the palate. Children should be given food that suits their temperament, prepared in a way that ensures hygiene and cleanliness, that is pleasant to the taste and yet very simple. This food should be chosen and apportioned according to the age of the child and his regular activities. It should contain all the chemical and dynamic elements that are necessary for his development and the balanced growth of every part of his body.

*

...one must strictly shun all excess and every vice, great or small; one must deny oneself the use of such slow poisons as tobacco, alcohol, etc., which men have a habit of developing into indispensable needs that gradually destroy the will and the memory. The all-absorbing interest which nearly all human beings, even the most intellectual, have in food, its preparation and its consumption, should be replaced by an almost chemical knowledge of the needs of the body and a very scientific austerity in satisfying them.

*

Physically, we depend upon food to live – unfortunately. For with food, we daily and constantly take in a formidable amount of inconscience, of *tamas*, heaviness, stupidity. One can't do otherwise – unless constantly, without a break, we remain completely aware and, as soon as an element is introduced into our body, we immediately work upon it to extract from it only the light and reject all that may darken our consciousness. This is the origin and rational explanation of the religious practice of consecrating one's food to God before taking it. When eating one aspires that this food may not be taken for the little human ego but as an offering to the divine consciousness within oneself. In all yogas, all religions, this is encouraged. This is the origin of that practice, of contacting the consciousness behind, precisely to diminish as much as possible the absorption of an inconscience which increases daily, constantly, without one's being aware of it.

*

One piece of advice given here is that one should always be kind. It should not be mistaken for the sort of advice people normally give. It says something interesting, even very interesting. My comment is: Always be kind and you will be free from suffering, always be contented and happy, and you will radiate your quiet happiness.

It is particularly noticeable that all the digestive functions are extremely sensitive to an attitude that is critical, bitter, full of ill-will, to a sour judgment. Nothing disturbs the functioning of the digestion more than that. And it is a vicious circle: the more the digestive function is disturbed, the more unkind you become, critical, dissatisfied with life and things and people. So you can't find any way out. And there is only one cure: to deliberately drop this attitude, to absolutely forbid yourself to have it and to impose upon yourself, by constant self-control, a deliberate attitude of all-comprehending kindness. Just try and you will see that you feel much better.

*

In Tokyo I had a garden and in this garden I was growing vegetables myself. I had a fairly big garden and many vegetables. And so, every morning I used to go for a walk, after having watered them and all the rest; I used to walk around to choose which vegetables I could take for eating. Well, just imagine! there were some which said to me, "No, no, no, no, no."... And then there were others which called, and I saw them from a distance, and they were saying, "Take me, take me, take me!" So it was very simple, I looked for those which wanted to be taken and never did I touch those which did not. I used to think it was something exceptional. I loved my plants very much, I used to look after them, I had put a lot of consciousness into them while watering them, cleaning them, so I thought they had a special capacity, perhaps.

But in France it was the same thing. I had a garden also in the south of France where I used to grow peas, radishes, carrots. Well, there were some which were happy, which asked to be taken and eaten, and there were those which said, "No, no, no, don't touch me, don't touch me!"

Pain, Illness and Accidents

Sri Aurobindo:

Your theory of illness is rather a perilous creed – for illness is a thing to be eliminated, not accepted or enjoyed. There is something in the being that enjoys illness, it is possible even to turn the pains of illness like any other pain into a form of pleasure; for pain and pleasure are both of them degradations of an original Ananda and can be reduced into the terms of each other or else sublimated into their original principle of Ananda. It is true also that one must be able to bear illness with calm, equanimity, endurance, even recognition of it, since it has come, as something that had to be passed through in the course of experience. But to accept and enjoy it means to help it to last and that will not do; for illness is a deformation of the physical nature just as lust, anger, jealousy, etc., are deformations of the vital nature and error and prejudice and indulgence of falsehood are deformations of the mental nature. All these things have to be eliminated and rejection is the first condition of their disappearance while acceptance has a contrary effect altogether.

*

Illness marks some imperfection or weakness or else opening to adverse touches in the physical nature and is often connected also with some obscurity or disharmony in the lower vital or the physical mind or elsewhere.

It is very good if one can get rid of illness entirely by faith and yoga-power or the influx of the Divine Force. But very often this is not altogether possible, because the whole nature is not open or able to respond to the Force. The mind may have faith and respond, but the lower vital and the body may not follow. Or, if the mind and vital are ready, the body may not respond, or may respond only partially, because it has the habit of replying to the forces which produce a particular illness, and habit is a very obstinate force in the material part of the nature. In such cases the use of the physical means can be resorted to, – not as the main means, but as a help or material support to the action of the Force. Not strong and violent remedies, but those that are beneficial without disturbing the body.

*

The Mother:
   I have told you first of all that all illness without any exception – without exception – is the expression of a break in equilibrium. But there are many kinds of breaks in equilibrium.... First, I am speaking only of the body, I am not speaking of the nervous illnesses of the vital or of mental illnesses. We shall see that later on. We are speaking only of this poor little body. And I say that all illnesses, all, whatever they may be (I would add even accidents) come from a break in equilibrium. That is, if all your organs, all the members and parts of your body are in harmony with one another, you are in perfect health. But if there is the slightest imbalance anywhere, immediately you get either just a little ill or quite ill, even very badly ill, or else an accident occurs. That always happens whenever there is an inner imbalance.

*

You must observe yourself a little and say that when you are afraid it is as though the fear was attracting the thing you are afraid of. If you are afraid of illness, it is as though you were attracting the illness. If you are afraid of an accident, it is as though you were attracting the accident. And if you look into yourself and around yourself a little, you will find it out, it is a persistent fact. So if you have just a little common sense, you say: "It is stupid to be afraid of anything, for it is precisely as though I were making a sign to that thing to come to me. If I had an enemy who wanted to kill me, I would not go and tell him: 'You know, it's me you want to kill!' " It is something like that. So since fear is bad, we won't have it. And if you say you are unable to prevent it by your reason, well, that shows you have no control over yourselves and must make a little effort to control yourselves. That is all.

*

How can one increase the receptivity of the body?

It depends on the part. The method is almost the same for all parts of the being. To begin with, the first condition: to remain as quiet as possible. You may notice that in the different parts of your being, when something comes and you do not receive it, this produces a shrinking – there is something which hardens in the vital, the mind or the body. There is a stiffening and this hurts, one feels a mental, vital or physical pain. So, the first thing is to put one's will and relax this shrinking , as one does a twitching nerve or a cramped muscle; you must learn how to relax, be able to relieve this tension in whatever part of the being it may be.

The method of relaxing the contraction may be different in the mind, the vital or the body, but logically it is the same thing. Once you have relaxed the tension, you see first if the disagreeable effect ceases, which would prove that it was a small momentary resistance, but if the pain continues and if it is indeed necessary to increase the receptivity in order to be able to receive what is helpful, what should be received, you must, after having relaxed this contraction, begin trying to widen yourself – you feel you are widening yourself. There are many methods. Some find it very useful to imagine they are floating on water with a plank under their back. Then they widen themselves, widen, until they become the vast liquid mass. Others make an effort to identify themselves with the sky and the stars, so they widen, widen themselves, identifying themselves more and more with the sky. Others again don't need these pictures; they can become conscious of their consciousness, enlarge their consciousness more and more until it becomes unlimited. One can enlarge it till it becomes vast as the earth and even the universe. When one does that one becomes really receptive.

*

...You are in pain, in great pain; it is hurting very much, you are suffering a lot.

First point: do not stress the pain by telling yourself, "Oh, how painful! Oh, this pain is unbearable! Oh, it is becoming worse and worse, I shall never be able to bear it", etc., all this sort of thing. The more you go on thinking like this and feeling like this and the more your attention is concentrated on it, the pain increases amazingly.

So, the first point: to control yourself sufficiently not to do that.

Second point: as I said, it depends on your habits. If you know how to concentrate, to be quiet, and if you can bring into yourself a certain peace, of any kind – it may be a mental peace, it may be a vital peace, it may be a psychic peace; they have different values and qualities, this is an individual question – you try to realise within yourself a state of peace or attempt to enter into a conscious contact with a force of peace.... Suppose you succeed more or less completely. Then, if you can draw the peace into yourself and bring it down into the solar plexus – for we are not talking of inner states but of your physical body – and from there direct it very calmly, very slowly I might say, but very persistently, towards the place where the pain is more or less sharp, and fix it there, this is very good.

This is not always enough.

But if by widening this movement you can add a sort of mental formation with a little life in it – not just cold, but with a little life in it – that the only reality is the divine Reality, and all the cells of this body are a more or less deformed expression of this divine Reality — there is only one Reality, the Divine, and our body is a more or less deformed expression of this sole Reality – if by my aspiration, my concentration, I can bring into the cells of the body the consciousness of this *sole* Reality, all disorder must necessarily cease.

*

What are the causes of accidents? Are they due to a disequilibrium?

...Outwardly there are many causes, but there is a deeper cause which is always there. I said the other day that if the nervous envelope is intact, accidents can be avoided, and even if there is an accident it won't have any consequences. As soon as there is a scratch or a defect in the nervous envelope of the being and according to the nature of this scratch, if one may say so, its place, its character, there will be an accident which will correspond to the diminution of resistance in the envelope. I believe almost everybody is psychologically aware of one thing: that accidents occur when one has a sort of uncomfortable feeling, when one is not fully conscious and self-possessed, when one feels uneasy. In any case, generally, people have a feeling that they are not fully themselves, not fully aware of what they are doing. If one were fully conscious, the consciousness wide awake, accidents would not occur; one would make just the right gesture, the necessary movement to avoid the accident. Hence, in an almost absolute way, it is a flagging of consciousness.

Death

Sri Aurobindo:

The soul takes birth each time, and each time a mind, life and body are formed out of the materials of universal nature according to the soul's past evolution and its need for the future.

When the body is dissolved, the vital goes into the vital plane and remains there for a time, but after a time the vital sheath disappears. The last to dissolve is the mental sheath. Finally the soul or psychic being retires into the psychic world to rest there till a new birth is close.

This is the general course for ordinarily developed human beings. There are variations according to the nature of the individual and his development. For example, if the mental is strongly developed, then the mental being can remain; so also can the vital, provided they are organized by and centred around the true psychic being; they share the immortality of the psychic.

The soul gathers the essential elements of its experiences in life and makes that its basis of growth in the evolution; when it returns to birth it takes up with its mental, vital, physical sheaths so much of its Karma as is useful to it in the new life for further experience.

It is really for the vital part of the being that śrāddha and rites are done – to help the being to get rid of the vital vibrations which still attach it to the earth or to the vital worlds, so that it may pass quickly to its rest in the psychic peace.

*

What has happened must now be accepted calmly as the thing decreed and best for his soul's progress from life to life, though not the best in human eyes which look only at the present and at outside appearance. For the spiritual seeker death is only a passage from one form of life to another, and none is dead but only departed. Look at it as that and shaking from you all reactions of vital grief, – that cannot help him in his journey, – pursue steadfastly the path to the Divine.

*

Sadhana has to be done in the body, it cannot be done by the soul without the body. When the body drops, the soul goes wandering in other worlds – and finally it comes back to another life and another body. Then all the difficulties it had not solved meet it again in the new life. So what is the use of leaving the body?

Moreover, if one throws away the body wilfully, one suffers much in the other worlds and when one is born again, it is in worse, not in better conditions.

The only sensible thing is to face the difficulties in this life and this body and conquer them.

*

The Mother:

...This is a question which every person whose consciousness is awakened a little has asked himself at least once in his life. There is in the depths of the being such a need to perpetuate, to prolong, to develop life, that the moment one has a first contact with death, which, although it may be quite an accidental contact, is yet inevitable, there is a sort of recoil in the being.

In persons who are sensitive, it produces horror; in others, indignation. There is a tendency to ask oneself: "What is this monstrous farce in which one takes part without wanting to, without understanding it? Why are we born, if it is only to die? Why all this effort for development, progress, the flowering of the faculties, if it is to come to a diminution ending in decline and disintegration?..." Some feel a revolt in them, others less strong feel despair and always this question arises: "If there is a conscious Will behind all that, this Will seems to be monstrous."

But here Sri Aurobindo tells us that this was an indispensable means of awakening in the consciousness of matter the need for perfection, the necessity of progress, that without this catastrophe, all beings would have been satisfied with the condition they were in – perhaps.... This is not certain.

*

...And after all, if one must for some reason or other leave one's body and take a new one, is it not better to make of one's death something magnificent, joyful, enthusiastic, than to make it a disgusting defeat? Those who cling on, who try by every possible means to delay the end even by a minute or two, who give you an example of frightful anguish, show that they are not conscious of their soul.... After all, it is perhaps a means, isn't it? One can change this accident into a means; if one is conscious one can make a beautiful thing of it, a very beautiful thing, as of everything. And note, those who do not fear it, who are not anxious, who can die without any sordidness are those who never think about it, who are not haunted all the time by this "horror" facing them which they must escape and which they try to push as far away from them as they can. These, when the occasion comes, can lift their head, smile and say, "Here I am."

It is they who have the will to make the best possible use of their life, it is they who say, "I shall remain here as long as it is necessary, to the last second, and I shall not lose one moment to realise my goal"; these, when the necessity comes, put up the best show. Why? – It is very simple, because they live in their ideal, the truth of their ideal; because that is the real thing for them, the very reason of their being, and in all things they can see this ideal, this reason of existence, and never do they come down into the sordidness of material life.

So, the conclusion:

One must never wish for death.

One must never will to die.

One must never be afraid to die.

And in all circumstances one must will to exceed oneself.

*

Mother, since in each new life the mind and vital as well as the body are new, how can the experiences of past lives be useful for them? Do we have to go through all the experiences once again?

That depends on people!

It is not the mind and vital which develop and progress from life to life – except in altogether exceptional cases and at a very advanced stage of evolution – it is the psychic. So, this is what happens: the psychic has alternate periods of activity and rest; it has a life of progress resulting from experiences of the physical life, of active life in a physical body, with all the experiences of the body, the vital and the mind; then, normally, the psychic goes into a kind of rest for assimilation where the result of the progress accomplished during its active existence is worked out, and when this assimilation is finished, when it has absorbed the progress it had prepared in its active life on earth, it comes down again in a new body bringing with it the result of all its progress and, at an advanced stage, it even chooses the environment and the kind of body and the kind of life in which it will live to complete its experience concerning one point or another. In some very advanced cases the psychic can, before leaving the body, decide what kind of life it will have in its next incarnation.

When it has become an almost completely formed and already very conscious being, it presides over the formation of the new body, and usually through an inner influence it chooses the element and the substance which will form its body in such a way that the body is adapted to the needs of its new experience. But this is at a rather advanced stage. And later, when it is fully formed and returns to earth with the idea of service, of collective help and participation in the Divine Work, then it is able to bring to the body in formation certain elements of the mind and vital from previous lives which, having been organised and impregnated with psychic forces in previous lives, could be preserved and, consequently, can participate in the general progress. But this is at a very, very advanced stage.

A True Friend

The Mother:

Now, at the beginning of the sentence I said, "He loves you in the best part of yourself...." To put it a little more positively: Your friend is not one who encourages you to come down to your lowest level, encourages you to do foolish things along with him or fall into bad ways with him or one who commends you for all the nasty things you do, that's quite clear. And yet, usually, very, very often, much too often, one makes friends with somebody with whom one doesn't feel uneasy when one has sunk lower. One considers as one's best friend somebody who encourages one in one's follies: one mixes with others to roam about instead of going to school, to go and steal fruit from gardens, to make fun of one's teachers and for all kinds of things like that. I am not making any personal remarks, but indeed I could quote some examples, unhappily far too many. And perhaps this is why I said, "They are not your true friends." But still, they are the most convenient friends, for they don't make you feel that you are in the wrong; while to one who comes and tells you, "Now then, instead of roaming about and doing nothing or doing stupid things, if you came to the class, don't you think it would be better!" usually one replies, "Don't bother me! you are not my friend." This is perhaps why I wrote this sentence. There you are. I repeat, I am not making any personal remarks, but still it is an opportunity to tell you something that unfortunately happens much too often.

There are children here who were full of promise, who

were at the top of their class, who used to work seriously, from whom I expected much, and who have been completely ruined by this kind of friendship. Since we are speaking of this, I shall tell them today that I regret this very much and that I do not call such people friends but mortal enemies against whom one should protect oneself as one would against a contagious disease.

We don't like the company of someone who has a contagious disease, and avoid him carefully; generally he is segregated so that it does not spread. But the contagion of vice and bad behaviour, the contagion of depravity, falsehood and what is base, is infinitely more dangerous than the contagion of any disease, and this is what must be very carefully avoided. You must consider as your best friend the one who tells you that he does not wish to participate in any bad or ugly act, the one who gives you courage to resist low temptations; he is a friend. He is the one you must associate with and not someone with whom you have fun and who strengthens your evil propensities.

*

Indeed, you should choose as friends only those who are wiser than yourself, those whose company ennobles you and helps you to master yourself, to progress, to act in a better way and see more clearly. And finally, the best friend one can have – isn't he the Divine, to whom one can say everything, reveal everything? For there indeed is the source of all compassion, of all power to efface every error when it is not repeated, to open the road to true realisation; it is he who can understand all, heal all, and always help on the path, help you not to fail, not to falter, not to fall, but to walk straight to the goal. He is the true friend, the friend of good and bad days, the one who can understand, can heal, and who is always there when you need him. When you call him sincerely, he is always there to guide and uphold you – and to love you in the true way.

Love

Sri Aurobindo:

I suppose "love" expresses something more intense than goodwill which can include mere liking or affection. But whether love or goodwill the human feeling is always either based on or strongly mixed with ego, – that is why it cannot be pure. It is said in the Upanishad, "One does not love the wife for the sake of the wife", or the child or friend etc. as the case may be, "but for one's self's sake one loves the wife". There is usually a hope of return, of benefit or advantage of some kind, or of certain pleasures and gratifications, mental, vital or physical that the person loved can give. Remove these things and the love very soon sinks, diminishes or disappears or turns into anger, reproach, indifference or even hatred. But there is also an element of habit, something that makes the presence of the person loved a sort of necessity because it has always been there – and this is sometimes so strong that even in spite of entire incompatibility of temper, fierce antagonism, something like hatred, it lasts and even these gulfs of discord are not enough to make the persons part; in other cases, this feeling is more tepid and after a time one gets accustomed to separation or accepts a substitute. There is again often the element of some kind of spontaneous attraction or affinity – mental, vital or physical, which gives a stronger cohesion to the love. Lastly, there is in the highest or deepest kind of love the psychic element which comes from the inmost heart and soul, a kind of inner union or self-giving or at least a seeking for that, a tie or an urge independent of other conditions or elements, existing for its own sake and not for any mental, vital or physical pleasure, satisfaction, interest or habit. But usually the psychic element in human love, even where it is present, is so much mixed, overloaded and hidden under the others that it has little chance of fulfilling itself or achieving its own natural purity and fullness. What is called love is therefore sometimes one thing, sometimes another, most often a confused mixture, and it is impossible to give a general answer to the questions you put as to what is meant by love in such and such a case. It depends on the persons and the circumstances.

When the love goes towards the Divine, there is still this ordinary human element in it. There is the call for a return and if the return does not seem to come, the love may sink; there is the self-interest, the demand for the Divine as a giver of all that the human being wants and, if the demands are not acceded to, *abhimāna* against the Divine, loss of faith, loss of fervour, etc., etc. But the true love for the Divine is in its fundamental nature not of this kind, but psychic and spiritual. The psychic element is the need of the inmost being for self-giving, love, adoration, union which can only be fully satisfied by the Divine. The spiritual element is the need of the being for contact, merging, union with its own highest and whole self and source of being and consciousness and bliss, the Divine. These two are two sides of the same thing. The mind, vital, physical can be the supports and recipients of this love, but they can be fully that only when they become remoulded in harmony with the psychic and spiritual elements of the being and no longer bring in the lower insistences of the ego.

*

The Mother:

The movement of love is not limited to human beings and it is perhaps less distorted in other worlds than in the human. Look at the flowers and trees. When the sun sets and all becomes silent, sit down for a moment and put yourself into communion with Nature: you will feel rising from the earth, from below the roots of the trees and mounting upward and coursing through their fibres, up to the highest outstretching branches, the aspiration of an intense love and longing, – a longing for something that brings light and gives happiness, for the light that is gone and they wish to have back again. There is a yearning so pure and intense that if you can feel the movement in the trees, your own being too will go up in an ardent prayer for the peace and light and love that are unmanifested here.

*

Love is universal and eternal; it is always manifesting itself and always identical in its essence. And it is a Divine Force; for the distortions we see in its apparent workings belong to its instruments. Love does not manifest in human beings alone; it is everywhere. Its movement is there in plants, perhaps in the very stones; in the animals it is easy to detect its presence. All the deformations of this great and divine Power come from the obscurity and ignorance and selfishness of the limited instrument. Love, the eternal force, has no clinging, no desire, no hunger for possession, no self-regarding attachment; it is, in its pure movement, the seeking for union of the self with the Divine, a seeking absolute and regardless of all other things. Love divine gives itself and asks for nothing. What human beings have made of it, we do not need to say; they have turned it into an ugly and repulsive thing. And yet even in human beings the first contact of love does bring down something of its purer substance; they become capable for a moment of forgetting themselves, for a moment its divine touch awakens and magnifies all that is fine and beautiful. But afterwards there comes to the surface the human nature, full of its impure demands, asking for something in exchange, bartering what it gives, clamouring for its own inferior satisfactions, distorting and soiling what was divine.

*

...the best way when love comes, in whatever form it may be, is to try and pierce through its outer appearance and find the divine principle which is behind and which gives it existence. Naturally, it is full of snares and difficulties, but it is more effective. That is to say, instead of ceasing to love because one loves wrongly, one must cease to love wrongly and want to love well.

For instance, love between human beings, in all its forms, the love of parents for children, of children for parents, of brothers and sisters, of friends and lovers, is all tainted with ignorance, selfishness and all the other defects which are man's ordinary drawbacks; so instead of completely ceasing to love – which, besides, is very difficult as Sri Aurobindo says, which would simply dry up the heart and serve no end – one must learn how to love better: to love with devotion, with self-giving, self-abnegation, and to struggle, not against love itself, but against its distorted forms: against all forms of monopolising, of attachment, possessiveness, jealousy, and all the feelings which accompany these main movements. Not to want to possess, to dominate; and not to want to impose one's will, one's whims, one's desires; not to want to take, to receive, but to give; not to insist on the other's response, but be content with one's own love; not to seek one's personal interest and joy and the fulfilment of one's personal desire, but to be satisfied with the giving of one's love and affection; and not to ask for any response. Simply to be happy to love, nothing more.

If you do that, you have taken a great stride forward and can, through this attitude, gradually advance farther in the feeling itself, and realise one day that love is not something personal, that love is a universal divine feeling which manifests through you more or less finely, but which in its essence is something divine.

Qualities of a Monitor and Instructor

Sri Aurobindo:

...More important still is the custom of discipline, obedience, order, habit of team-work, which certain games necessitate. For without them success is uncertain or impossible. Innumerable are the activities in life, especially in national life, in which leadership and obedience to leadership in combined action are necessary for success, victory in combat or fulfilment of a purpose. The role of the leader, the captain, the power and skill of his leadership, his ability to command the confidence and ready obedience of his followers is of the utmost importance in all kinds of combined action or enterprise; but few can develop these things without having learnt themselves to obey and to act as one mind or as one body with others. This strictness of training, this habit of discipline and obedience is not inconsistent with individual freedom; it is often the necessary condition for its right use, just as order is not inconsistent with liberty but rather the condition for the right use of liberty and even for its preservation and survival. In all kinds of concerted action this rule is indispensable: orchestration becomes necessary and there could be no success for an orchestra in which individual musicians played according to their own fancy and refused to follow the indications of the conductor.

*

The Mother:

Personality Traits of a Successful Teacher

1. Complete self-control not only to the extent of not showing any anger, but remaining absolutely quiet and undisturbed under all circumstances.

2. In the matter of self-confidence, must also have a sense of the relativity of his importance.

   Above all, must have the knowledge that the teacher himself must always progress if he wants his students to progress, must not remain satisfied either with what he is or with what he knows.

3. Must not have any sense of essential superiority over his students nor preference or attachment whatsoever for one or another.

4. Must know that all are equal spiritually and instead of mere tolerance must have a global comprehension or understanding.

*

Is it possible to teach the ideal to those who do not understand it, and how can it be taught to them? Are we, instuctors and teachers, worthy of this formidable task?

What we want to teach is not only a mental ideal, it is a new idea of life and a realisation of consciousness. This realisation is new to all, and the only true way to teach others is to live according to this new consciousness oneself and to allow oneself to be tranformed by it. There is no better lesson than that of an example. To tell others: "Do not be selfish," is not much use, but if somebody is free from all selfishness, he becomes a wonderful example to others; and someone who sincerely aspires to act in accordance with the Supreme Truth, creates a kind of contagion for the people around him. So the first duty of all those who are teachers or instructors is to give an example of the qualities they teach to others.

And if, among these teachers and instructors, some are not worthy of their post, because by their character they give a bad example, their first duty is to become worthy by changing their character and their action; there is no other way.

*

...as a general and absolute rule, the teachers and especially the physical education instructors must be a constant living example of the qualities demanded from the students; discipline, regularity, good manners, courage, endurance, patience in effort, are taught much more by example than by words. And as an absolute rule: never to do in front of a child what you forbid him to do.

For the rest, each case implies its own solution, and one must act with tact and discernment.

That is why to be a teacher or an instructor is the best of all disciplines, if one knows how to comply with it.

Freedom and Discipline

The Mother:

But what is very important is to know what you want. And for this a minimum of freedom is necessary. You must not be under a compulsion or an obligation. You must be able to do things whole-heartedly. If you are lazy, well, you will know what it means to be lazy.... You know, in life idlers are obliged to work ten times more than others, for what they do they do badly, so they are obliged to do it again. But these are things one must learn by experience. They can't be instilled into you.

The mind, if not controlled, is something wavering and imprecise. If one doesn't have the habit of concentrating it upon something, it goes on wandering all the time. It goes on without a stop anywhere and wanders into a *world* of vagueness. And then, when one wants to fix one's attention, it hurts! There is a little effort there, like this: "Oh! how tiring it is, it hurts!" So one does not do it. And one lives in a kind of cloud. And your head is like a cloud; it's like that, most brains are like clouds: there is no precision, no exactitude, no clarity, it is hazy – vague and hazy. You have impressions rather than a knowledge of things. You live in an approximation, and you can keep within you all sorts of contradictory ideas made up mostly of impressions, sensations, feelings, emotions – all sorts of things like that which have very little to do with thought and... which are just vague ramblings.

But if you want to succeed in having a precise, concrete, clear, definite thought on a certain subject, you must make an effort, gather yourself together, hold yourself firm, concentrate. And the first time you do it, it literally hurts, it is tiring! But if you don't make a habit of it, all your life you will be living in a state of irresolution. And when it comes to practical things, when you are faced with – for, in spite of everything, one is always faced with – a number of problems to solve, of a very practical kind, well, instead of being able to take up the elements of the problem, to put them all face to face, look at the question from every side, and rising above and seeing the solution, instead of that you will be tossed about in the swirls of something grey and uncertain, and it will be like so many spiders running around in your head – but you won't succeed in catching the thing.

I am speaking of the simplest of problems, you know; I am not speaking of deciding the fate of the world or humanity, or even of a country – nothing of the kind. I am speaking of the problems of your daily life, of every day. They become something quite woolly.

Well, it is to avoid this that you are told, when your brain is in course of being formed, "Instead of letting it be shaped by such habits and qualities, try to give it a little exactitude, precision, capacity of concentration, of choosing, deciding, putting things in order, try to use your reason."

*

...I have said and I repeat that if a student feels quite alien to a subject, for example, if a student feels he has an ability for literature and poetry and has a distaste or at least an indifference for mathematics, if he tells me, "I prefer not to follow the mathematics course", I can't tell him, "No, it is absolutely necessary to go to it." But if a student has decided to follow a class, it is an absolutely *elementary* discipline that he follows it, goes to it regularly and behaves himself properly there; otherwise he is *altogether unworthy* of going to school. I have never encouraged anyone to roam about during class-hours and to come one day and be absent the next, never, for, to begin with, if he can't submit to this quite elementary discipline, he will never acquire the least control over himself, he will always be the slave of all his impulses and all his fancies.

If you don't want to study a certain branch of knowledge, that is all right, no one can compel you to do it; but if you decide to do something – anything in life, if you decide to do a thing – you must do it *honestly*, with discipline, regularity and method. And without whims. I have never approved of anyone being the plaything of his own impulses and fancies, never, and you will never be able to have that from me, for then one is no longer a human being, one is an animal. So, here is one of the questions quite settled, without any discussion.

*

True strength and protection come from the Divine Presence in the heart.

If you want to keep this Presence constantly in you, avoid carefully all vulgarity in speech, behaviour and acts.

Do not mistake liberty for license and freedom for bad manners: the thoughts must be pure and the aspiration ardent.

*

To the students
To be noisy in class is an act of selfish stupidity.
If you don't intend to attend the class silently and attentively, it is better not to come.

*

It is forbidden to fight at school, to fight in class, to fight in the playground, to fight in the street, to fight at home (whether at your parents' house or in a boarding).

Always and everywhere children are forbidden to fight among themselves, for each time that one gives a blow to another, one gives it to one's own soul.

*

I insist on the necessity of having good manners. I do not see anything grand in the manners of a gutter-snipe.

Choice of Books

The Mother:

Once or twice, as a game, you took one of your books or Sri Aurobindo's and opened a page at random, and read out a sentence. Can these sentences give one a sign or an indication? What should we do to get a true answer?

Everybody can do it. It is done in this way: you concentrate. Now, it depends on what you want. If you have an inner problem and want the solution, you concentrate on this problem; if you want to know the condition you are in, which you are not aware of – if you want to get some light on the state you are in, you just come forward with simplicity and ask for the light. Or else, quite simply, if you are curious to know what the invisible knowledge has to tell you, you remain silent and still for a moment and then open the book. I always used to recommend taking a paper-knife, because it is thinner; while you are concentrated you insert it in the book and with the tip indicate something. Then, if you know how to concentrate, that is to say, if you really do it with an aspiration to have an answer, it always comes.

For, in books of this kind (*Mother shows* The Synthesis of Yoga), books of revelation, there is always an accumulation of forces – at least of higher mental forces, and most often of spiritual forces of the highest knowledge. Every book, on account of the words it contains, is like a small accumulator of these forces. People don't know this, for they don't know how to make use of it, but it is so. In the same way, in every picture, photograph, there is an accumulation, a small accumulation representative of the force of the person whose picture it is, of his nature and, if he has powers, of his powers. Now, you, when you are sincere and have an aspiration, you emanate a certain vibration, the vibration of your aspiration which goes and meets the corresponding force in the book, and it is a higher consciousness which gives you the answer.

Everything is contained potentially. Each element of a whole potentially contains what is in the whole. It is a little difficult to explain, but you will understand with an example: when people want to practise magic, if they have a bit of nail or hair, it is enough for them, because within this, potentially, there is all that is in the being itself. And in a book there is potentially – not expressed, not manifest – the knowledge which is in the person who wrote the book. Thus, Sri Aurobindo represented a totality of comprehension and knowledge and power; and every one of his books is at once a symbol and a representation. Every one of his books contains symbolically, potentially, what is in him. Therefore, if you concentrate on the book, you can, through the book, go back to the source. And even, by passing through the book, you will be able to receive much more than what is just in the book.

There is always a way of reading and understanding what one reads, which gives an answer to what you want. It is not just a chance or an amusement, nor is it a kind of diversion. You may do it just "like that", and then nothing at all happens to you, you have no reply and it is not interesting. But if you do it seriously, if seriously your aspiration tries to concentrate on this instrument – it is like a battery, isn't it, which contains energies – if it tries to come into contact with the energy which is there and insists on having the answer to what it wants to know, well, naturally, the energy which is there – the union of the two forces, the force given out by you and that accumulated in the book – will guide your hand and your paper-knife or whatever you have; it will guide you exactly to the thing that expresses what you ought to know.... Obviously, if one does it without sincerity or conviction, nothing at all happens. If it is done sincerely, one gets an answer.

Certain books are like this, more powerfully charged than others; there are others where the result is less clear. But generally, books containing aphorisms and short sentences — not very long philosophical explanations, but rather things in a condensed and precise form – it is with these that one succeeds best.

Naturally, the value of the answer depends on the value of the spiritual force contained in the book. If you take a novel, it will tell you nothing at all but stupidities. But if you take a book containing a condensation of forces – of knowledge or spiritual force or teaching power – you will receive your answer.

*

You can read sacred books and yet be far away from the Divine; and you can read the most stupid productions and be in touch with the Divine. It is not possible to get an idea of what the transformed consciousness and its movements are until you have had a taste of the transformation. There is a way of consciousness in union with the Divine in which you can enjoy all you read, as you can all you observe, even the most indifferent books or the most uninteresting things. You can hear poor music, even music from which one would like to run away, and yet you can, not for its outward self but because of what is behind, enjoy it. You do not lose the distinction between good music and bad music, but you pass through either into that which it expresses. For there is nothing in the world which has not its ultimate truth and support in the Divine. And if you are not stopped by the appearance, physical or moral or aesthetic, but get behind and are in touch with the Spirit, the Divine Soul in things, you can reach beauty and delight even through what affects the ordinary sense only as something poor, painful or discordant.

*

Don't you think there are enough ugly things in the world without one's giving a picture of them in books? This is something which always used to surprise me, even when I was a child – life is so ugly, so full of mean, miserable, even at times repulsive things, what is the use of imagining yet worse things than are already there? If you imagined something more beautiful, a more beautiful life, that would be worth the trouble. People who take pleasure in writing ugly things show a great poverty of mind – it is always a sign of a poverty of mind. It is infinitely more difficult to tell a story beautiful from beginning to end than to write a story ending with a sensational event or a catastrophe. Many authors, if they had to write a story which ends happily, beautifully, would not be able to do it – they do not have enough imagination for that. Very few stories have an uplifting ending, almost all end in a failure – for a very simple reason, it is much more easy to fall than to rise. It is much more difficult to end one's story on a note of greatness and splendour, to make one's hero a genius seeking to transcend himself, because for that one must be a genius oneself, and this is not given to everybody.

*

[*A teacher suggested that books dealing with subjects like crime, violence and licentiousness should not be available to young people.*]

It is not so much a question of subject-matter but of vulgarity of mind and narrowness and selfish common-sense in the conception of life, expressed in a form devoid of art, greatness or refinement, which must be carefully removed from the reading-matter of children both big and small. All that lowers and degrades the consciousness must be excluded.

Some Practical Advice

The Mother:

For those who want always to progress, there are three major ways of progressing:

1) To widen the field of one's consciousness.
2) To understand ever better and more completely what one knows.
3) To find the Divine and surrender more and more to his Will.

In other words, this means:

1) To constantly enrich the possibilities of the instrument.
2) To ceaselessly perfect the functioning of this instrument.
3) To make this instrument increasingly receptive and obedient to the Divine.

To learn to understand and do more and more things. To purify oneself of all that prevents one from being totally surrendered to the Divine. To make one's consciousness more and more receptive to the Divine Influence.

One could say: to widen oneself more and more, to deepen oneself more and more, to surrender oneself more and more completely.

*

*What is the meaning of one's birthday, apart from its com-
memorative character? How can one take advantage of this
occasion?*

Because of the rhythm of the universal forces, a person is
supposed to have a special receptivity on his birthday each
year.

He can therefore take advantage of this receptivity by
making good resolutions and fresh progress on the path of
his integral development.

*

Not to take care of material things which one uses is a
sign of inconscience and ignorance.

You have no right to use any material object whatsoever if
you do not take care of it.

You must take care of it not because you are attached to it,
but because it manifests something of the Divine Consciousness.

*

Thus before you eat, concentrate a few seconds in the aspiration that the food you are about to eat may bring your
body the substance it needs to serve as solid basis for your
effort towards the great discovery, and give it the energy for
persistence and perseverance in the effort.

Before you go to sleep, concentrate a few seconds in the
aspiration that the sleep may restore your fatigued nerves,
bring calm and quietness to your brain so that on waking you
may, with renewed vigour, begin again your journey on the

path of the great discovery....

When you speak, before the words come out of your mouth, concentrate just long enough to check your words and allow only those that are absolutely necessary to pass, only those that are not in any way harmful to your progress on the path of the great discovery....

To sum up, never forget the purpose and goal of your life.

*

Replace the ambition to be first by the will to do the best possible.

Replace the desire for success by the yearning for progress.

Replace the eagerness for fame by the aspiration for perfection.

Physical Education is meant to bring into the body, consciousness and control, discipline and mastery, all things necessary for a higher and better life.

Keep all that in mind, practise sincerely and you will become a good athlete; this is the first step on the way to be a true man.

*

...Someone comes and insults you or says unpleasant things to you; and if you begin to vibrate in unison with this anger or this ill-will, you feel quite weak and powerless and usually you make a fool of yourself. But if you manage to keep within yourself, especially in your head, a complete immobility which refuses to receive these vibrations, then at the same time you feel a great strength, and the other person cannot disturb you. If you remain very quiet, even physically, and when violence is directed at you, you are able to remain very quiet, very silent, very still, well, that has a power not only over you but over the other person also. If you don't have these vibrations of inner response, if can remain absolutely immobile within yourself, everywhere this has an almost immediate effect upon the other person.

That gives you an idea of the power of immobility. And it is a very common fact which can occur every day; it is not a great event of spiritual life, it is something of the outer, material life.

There is a tremendous power in immobility: mental immobility, sensorial immobility, physical immobility. If you can remain like a wall, absolutely motionless, everything the other person sends you will immediately fall back upon him. And it has an immediate action. It can stop the arm of the assassin, you understand, it has that strength. Only, one must not just appear to be immobile and yet be boiling inside! That's not what I mean. I mean an integral immobility.

*

...True quietude is a very great force, a very great strength. In fact one can say, looking at the problem from the other side, that all those who are really strong, powerful, are always very calm. It is only the weak who are agitated; as soon as one becomes truly strong, one is peaceful, calm, quiet, and one has the power of endurance to face the adverse waves which come rushing from outside in the hope of disturbing one. This true quietude is always a sign of force. Calmness belongs to the strong.

And this is true even in the physical field. I don't know if you have observed animals like lions, tigers, elephants, but it is a fact that when they are not in action, they are always so perfectly still. A lion sitting and looking at you always seems to be telling you, "Oh, how fidgety you are!" It looks at you with such a peaceful air of wisdom! And all its power, energy, physical strength are there, gathered, collected, concentrated and – without a shadow of agitation – ready for action when the order is given.

*

I suggest the same remedy as the one I was using in my childhood when disagreeing with my young playmates. I was at that time... very sensitive and I felt hurt when abused by them, especially by those whom I had shown only sympathy and kindness. I used to tell myself: "Why be sorry and feel miserable? If they are right in what they say, I have only to be glad for the lesson and correct myself; if they are wrong, why should I worry about it – it is for them to be sorry for their mistake. In both cases the best and the most dignified thing I can do is to remain strong, quiet and unmoved."

This lesson which I was giving myself and trying to follow when I was eight years old, still holds good in all similar cases.

*

To learn to be quiet and silent... When you have a problem to solve, instead of turning over in your head all the possibilities, all the consequences, all the possible things one should or should not do, if you remain quiet with an aspiration for goodwill, if possible a need for goodwill, the solution comes very quickly. And as you are silent you are able to hear it.

When you are caught in a difficulty, try this method: instead of becoming agitated, turning over all the ideas and actively seeking solutions, of worrying, fretting, running here and there inside your head – I don't mean externally, for externally you probably have enough common sense not to do that! But inside, in your head – *remain quiet*. And according to your nature, with ardour or peace, with intensity or widening or with all these together, implore the Light and wait for it to come.

In this way the path would be considerably shortened.

*

...So if you never go beyond the limit you have reached, you will never progress. It is quite obvious that people who practise physical culture, for example, if they make progress, it is just because they gradually exceed, go beyond what they could do.

It is all a matter of balance. And the period of receptivity should be in proportion to the period of expenditure.

But if one confines oneself to what one can do at a given moment... First of all it is impossible, for if one doesn't progress, one falls back. Therefore, one must *always* make a little effort to do a little more than before. Then one is on the upward path. If one is afraid of doing too much, one is sure to go down again and lose one's capacities.

One must always try a little more, a little better than one did the day before or the previous moment. Only, the more one increases one's effort, the more should one increase one's capacity of receptivity and the opportunities to receive. For instance, from the purely physical point of view, if one wants to develop one's muscles, a progressive effort must be made by them, that is to say, a greater and greater effort, but at the same time one must do what is needed: massage, hydrotherapy, etc. to increase at the same time their capacity to receive.

*

...If you have a tamasic nature, you must use another procedure. You must exert your consciousness, your will, your force, gather your energy, shake yourself a little and whip yourself and say: "Clac! clac! forward, march." If it is laziness that keeps you back from, say, doing the vaulting, you must immediately do something much more tiring and say: "Well, you don't want to do that? All right, you are going to do 1500 meters running!" Or else: "I don't want to do the weight-lifting today, I don't feel like doing it: good, I shall go skipping 4000 times at a stretch."

The same method should be used for studies also?

Yes, exactly. If you don't feel like learning your lesson, you take a book ten times more tiring, something dry and compel yourself to read it with attention. There are books of this kind, so dry, of such an arid kind of knowledge... Well, if you don't feel like reading your book of history or geography, which are after all very easy and very entertaining, instead of that take one of those books that are given to you *(Mother looks at a teacher)* – I do not dare to say anything, because your teacher is there! – extremely arid, and compel yourself to study at least half the book. Afterwards, everything else appears charming to you.

*

I suggest that every one of you should try – oh! not for long, just for one hour a day – to say nothing but the absolutely indispensable words. Not one more, not one less.

Take one hour of your life, the one which is most convenient for you, and during that time observe yourself closely and say only the absolutely indispensable words.

At the outset, the first difficulty will be to know what is absolutely indispensable and what is not. It is already a study in itself and every day you will do better.

Next, you will see that so long as one says nothing, it is not difficult to remain absolutely silent, but as soon as you begin to speak, always or almost always you say two or three or ten or twenty useless words which it was not at all necessary to say.

*

When you have a little time, whether it is one hour or a few minutes, tell yourself, "At last, I have some time to concentrate, to collect myself, to relive the purpose of my life, to offer myself to the True and the Eternal." If you took care to do this each time you are not harassed by outer circumstances, you would find out that you were advancing very quickly on the path. Instead of wasting your time in chattering, in doing useless things, reading things that lower the consciousness – to choose only the best cases, I am not speaking of other imbecilities which are much more serious – instead of trying to make yourself giddy, to make time, that is already so short, still shorter only to realise at the end of your life that you have lost three-quarters of your chance – then you want to put in double time, but that does not work – it is better to be moderate, balanced, patient, quiet, but never to lose an opportunity that is given to you, that is to say, to utilise for the true purpose the unoccupied moment before you.

When you have nothing to do, you become restless, you run about, you meet friends, you take a walk, to speak only of the best; I am not referring to things that are obviously not to be done. Instead of that, sit down quietly before the sky, before the sea or under trees, whatever is possible (here you have all of them) and try to realise one of these things – to understand why you live, to learn how you must live, to ponder over what you want to do and what should be done, what is the best way of escaping from the ignorance and falsehood and pain in which you live.

References

Booklet
Pages

1a. Bande Mataram, Cent. Ed. Vol.1, pp.516-517
1b. The Supramental Manifestation, Cent. Ed. Vol.16, pp.329-331
4.   Karmayogin, Cent. Ed. Vol.2, pp.20-21
5a. Words of the Mother, Cent. Ed. Vol.13, p.377
5b. On Education, Cent. Ed. Vol.12, p.259
6.   Questions and Answers, Cent. Ed. Vol. 3, p.238
7.   On Education, Cent. Ed. Vol.12, p.116
8a. On Education, Cent. Ed. Vol.12, p.3
8b. Some Answers from the Mother, Cent. Ed. Vol.16, pp.426-427
9a. Questions and Answers 1954, Cent. Ed. Vol.6, p.16
9b. Words of Long Ago, Cent. Ed. Vol.2, p.51
11a. Questions and Answers 57-58, Cent. Ed. Vol.9, pp.158-159
11b. Questions and Answers, Cent. Ed. Vol.3, p.2
12. Questions and Answers 50-51, Cent. Ed. Vol.4, pp.33-37
16. Questions and Answers 50-51, Cent. Ed. Vol.4, pp.117-119
18. Questions and Answers, Cent. Ed. Vol.3, p.215
19. On Education, Cent. Ed. Vol.12, pp.33-34
20a. Questions and Answers1954, Cent. Ed. Vol.6, pp.153-154
20b. Some Answers from the Mother, Cent. Ed.Vol.16, p.121
21. Questions and Answers1954, Cent. Ed. Vol.6, pp.18-20
24a. Questions and Answers, Cent. Ed. Vol.3, p.228
24b. On Education, Cent. Ed. Vol.12, pp.73-74
26. Questions and Answers1953, Cent. Ed. Vol.5, pp.127-128
29. The Synthesis of Yoga, Cent. Ed. Vol.20, pp.491-493
31. The Synthesis of Yoga, Cent. Ed.Vol.20, pp.132-133
32a. The hour of God, Cent. Ed. Vol.17, p.238
32b. The hour of God, Cent. Ed. Vol.17, p.247
33a. The hour of God, Cent. Ed. Vol.17, pp.245-246
33b. The hour of God, Cent. Ed. Vol.17, p.221
33c. On Education, Cent. Ed. Vol.12, p.138
34a. On Education, Cent. Ed. Vol.12, p.248

34b. Questions and Answers 57-58, Cent. Ed. Vol.9, p.239
35a. On Education, Cent. Ed. Vol.12, p.249
35b. On Education, Cent. Ed. Vol.12, p.249
35c. On Education, Cent. Ed. Vol.12, p.249
36a. On Education, Cent. Ed. Vol.12, pp.242-243
36b. Questions and Answers 1956, Cent. Ed. Vol.8, pp.236-237
36c. On Education, Cent. Ed. Vol.12, p.416
38a. The Supramental Manifestation, Cent. Ed. Vol.16, p.1
38b. The Supramental Manifestation, Cent. Ed. Vol.16, pp.2-3
 39. On Education, Cent. Ed. Vol.12, p.278
40a. On Education, Cent. Ed. Vol.12, p.278
40b. On Education, Cent. Ed. Vol.12, p.15
 41. On Education, Cent. Ed. Vol.12, p.51
42a. On Education, Cent. Ed. Vol.12, pp.289-290
42b. Questions and Answers 57-58, Cent. Ed. Vol.9, pp.96-97
 43. Questions and Answers 50-51, Cent. Ed. Vol.4, p.42
 44. Some Answers from the Mother, Cent. Ed. Vol.16, pp.397-398
45a. On Education, Cent. Ed. Vol.12, p.6
45b. White Roses, Ed.1980, pp.188-189
46a. Questions and Answers 50-51, Cent. Ed. Vol.4, p.24
46b. Questions and Answers 50-51, Cent. Ed. Vol.3, p.279
 47. Questions and Answers 50-51, Cent. Ed. Vol.4, pp.247-251
 51. Questions and Answers 1954, Cent. Ed. Vol.6, pp.78-80
54a. Letters on Yoga, Cent. Ed. Vol.24, p.1277
54b. Letters on Yoga, Cent. Ed. Vol.24, p.1279
54c. Letters on Yoga, Cent. Ed. Vol.24, p.1277
54d. Letters on Yoga, Cent. Ed. Vol.24, p.1278
54e. Questions and Answers, Cent. Ed. Vol.9, pp.100-102
 56. On Education, Cent. Ed.Vol.12, pp.5-6
 57. Questions and Answers 50-51, Cent. Ed. Vol.4, pp.335-336
 58. Questions and Answers, Cent. Ed. Vol.3, pp.195-196
 60. On Education, Cent. Ed. Vol.12, pp.4-5
61a. On Education, Cent. Ed. Vol.12, p.30
61b. On Education, Cent. Ed. Vol.12, pp.32-33
 63. Some Answers from the Mother, Cent. Ed. Vol.16, p.397

64. Questions and Answers 57-58, Cent. Ed. Vol.9, pp.360-361

65a. Questions and Answers 50-51, Cent. Ed. Vol.4, p.5

65b. Questions and Answers 50-51, Cent. Ed. Vol.4, pp.137-138

66. Questions and Answers 1954, Cent. Ed. Vol.6, pp.151-152

69a. On Education, Cent. Ed. Vol.12, p.53

69b. Questions and Answers 1956, Cent. Ed. Vol.8, pp.160-161

70a. Questions and Answers, Cent. Ed. Vol.3, pp.8-9

70b. Questions and Answers 50-51, Cent. Ed. Vol.4, pp.363-365

72. Questions and Answers 1953, Cent. Ed. Vol.5, pp.121-122

73. On Education, Cent. Ed. Vol.12, p.52

74a. On Education, Cent. Ed. Vol.12, p.160

74b. Some Answers from the Mother, Cent. Ed. Vol.15, pp.142-43

75a. Some Answers from the Mother, Cent. Ed. Vol.16, p.400

75b. Words of Long Ago, Cent. Ed. Vol.2, pp. 31-32

76a. Some Answers from the Mother, Cent. Ed. Vol. 16, pp.317-318

78a. Letters on Yoga, Cent. Ed. Vol.24, p.1467

78b. Letters on Yoga, Cent. Ed. Vol.24, p.1465

78c. On Education, Cent. Ed. Vol.12, pp.13-14

79. On Education, Cent. Ed. Vol.12, pp.51-52

80a. Questions and Answers 50-51, Cent. Ed. Vol.4, pp.334-335

80b. Questions and Answers, Cent. Ed. Vol.3, p.292

81. Questions and Answers 1954, Cent. Ed. Vol.6, pp.181-182

82a. Letters on Yoga, Cent. Ed. Vol.24, p.1566

82b. Letters on Yoga, Cent. Ed. Vol.24, p.1568

83. Questions and Answers 1953, Cent. Ed. Vol.5, p.173

84a. Questions and Answers 1953, Cent. Ed. Vol.5, p.318

84b. Questions and Answers 50-51, Cent. Ed. Vol.4, pp.265-266

85. Questions and Answers 1956, Cent. Ed. Vol.8, pp.213-214

87. Questions and Answers 50-51, Cent. Ed. Vol.4, pp.272-273

88. Letters on Yoga, Cent. Ed. Vol.22, p.433

89a. Letters on Yoga, Cent. Ed. Vol.22, pp.462-463

89b. Letters on Yoga, Cent. Ed. Vol.24, pp.1699-1700

89c. Questions and Answers 57-58, Cent. Ed. Vol.9, p.33

90. Questions and Answers 50-51, Cent. Ed. Vol.4, pp.355-356

91. Questions and Answers 57-58, Cent. Ed. Vol.9, pp.268-269

93.   Questions and Answers 57-58, Cent. Ed. Vol.9, pp.55-56
94.   Questions and Answers 57-58, Cent. Ed. Vol.9, p.57
96.   Letters on Yoga, Cent. Ed. Vol.23, pp.759-760
98a. Questions and Answers, Cent. Ed. Vol.3, p.72
98b. Questions and Answers, Cent. Ed. Vol.3, pp.69-70
99.   Questions and Answers 1956, Cent. Ed. Vol.8, pp.302-303
101. The Supramental Manifestation, Cent. Ed. Vol.16, p.3
102a. On Education, Cent. Ed. Vol.12, p.168
102b. On Education, Cent. Ed. Vol.12, pp.359-360
103. On Education, Cent. Ed. Vol.12, pp.363-364
104. Questions and Answers 1956, Cent. Ed. Vol.8, pp.182-183
105. Questions and Answers 1956, Cent. Ed. Vol.8, pp.356-357
106. On Education, Cent. Ed. Vol.12, p.155
107a. On Education, Cent. Ed. Vol.12, p.156
107b. On Education, Cent. Ed. Vol.12, p.156
107c. On Education, Cent. Ed. Vol.12, pp.154-155
108. Questions and Answers 1956, Cent. Ed. Vol.8, pp.163-165
110. Questions and Answers, Cent. Ed. Vol.3, p.27
111. Questions and Answers 50-51, Cent. Ed. Vol.4, p.155
112. On Education, Cent. Ed. Vol.12, p.147
113. Some Answers from the Mother, Cent. Ed. Vol.16, pp.433-434
114a. Some Answers from the Mother, Cent. Ed. Vol.16, p.310
114b. Words of the Mother, Cent. Ed. Vol.14, p.345
114c. On Education, Cent. Ed. Vol.12, p.34
115a. On Education, Cent. Ed. Vol.12, pp.275-276
115b. Questions and Answers 1956, Cent. Ed. Vol.8, pp.67-68
116. Questions and Answers 1956, Cent.Ed. Vol.8, pp.330-331
117a. On Education, Cent. Ed. Vol.12, p.157
117b. Questions and Answers 57-58, Cent. Ed. Vol.9, pp.423-424
118. Questions and Answers 1956, Cent. Ed. Vol.8, p.196
119. Questions and Answers 1953, Cent. Ed. Vol.5, pp.120-121
120a. Questions and Answers, Cent. Ed. Vol.3, p.259
120b. Questions and Answers, Cent. Ed. Vol.3, pp.250-251